"I expected this book to be good but found it to be great. *Conscience* is a much-needed treatment of a vital yet neglected subject. Naselli and Crowley's overview of the New Testament doctrine of conscience is superb. I was ready to say that that chapter was worth the price of the book, but in fact, I found every chapter to be worth the price of the book! Its treatment of how Christian consciences overlap yet differ and of why we need to calibrate our consciences was remarkable. This book is for everyone with an interest in cross-cultural ministry, as well as for those seeking to become all things to all people that they may win some. It's also extremely helpful for those living in churches, marriages, and friendships where different convictions aren't always as black-and-white as we imagine. *Conscience* would be great to study in a small group."

Randy Alcorn, Founder and Director, Eternal Perspective Ministries; author, *Heaven* and *Happiness*

"How should Christians navigate the complex world of disagreements with other Christians? Can we differentiate the scriptural nonnegotiables, the things we just personally feel strongly about, and those to which we give scarcely a second thought? How can the church best model unity in both love and truth in these matters? Naselli and Crowley bring both cross-cultural experience and scriptural acumen to deftly deal with these issues in straightforward language that almost anyone can grasp. Warmly recommended."

Craig L. Blomberg, Distinguished Professor of New Testament, Denver Seminary

"In our culture awash with instructions to follow our own hearts, we desperately need this book. On a personal note, next to the doctrine of the sovereignty of God, the Bible's teaching on the conscience has become to me a deeply encouraging motivation in my evangelism. In the last chapter in particular, Naselli and Crowley have given a great gift to cross-cultural workers everywhere!"

Gloria Furman, pastor's wife, Redeemer Church of Dubai; author, *The Pastor's Wife* and *Missional Motherhood*

D0369568

"It is rare to find a book that is both punchy and practical. It was a delight to read, and now it is a delight to recommend. I believe that the scriptural concept of the conscience has become so fuzzy or forgotten that *all* readers will find this little book illuminating for issues that touch upon *all* of life. All will find it life-giving. Some will find it life-changing."

Jason C. Meyer, Pastor for Preaching and Vision, Bethlehem Baptist Church, Minneapolis, Minnesota

"I have never read a better book on the conscience. Naselli and Crowley base their view of conscience on a careful reading of the Scriptures. At the same time, the book is full of practical wisdom. The biblical teaching on conscience is applied to numerous situations so that readers see how the Scriptures apply to everyday life. The reflections on how conscience should operate in missionary situations is alone worth the price of the book, but the entire book is a gem."

Thomas R. Schreiner, James Buchanan Harrison Professor of New Testament Interpretation and Associate Dean of the School of Theology, The Southern Baptist Theological Seminary

"There is, for too many of us, a casual, maybe even self-righteous, contentment with the current status of our consciences rather than an active cultivating of them so as to bring them more in line with God's view of things. This book pushes us to that second, better choice. It is a thoughtful and provocative treatment of this hugely important and all too often insufficiently considered subject. I believe you will find it very helpful."

Mike Bullmore, Senior Pastor, CrossWay Community Church, Bristol, Wisconsin

"Naselli and Crowley have produced a book of deep and broad practical relevance for living the Christian life. We are often far too little aware of the role of our consciences in our day-to-day lives, while the truth is, God has given us those faculties as part of the divinely designed means to keep us on the path of righteousness. I found their discussion of the recalibration of the conscience, and of how to deal with fellow Christians who have different senses of right and wrong, to be filled with biblical wisdom and enormous insight. Here is a book that promises great reward for those who will follow not only its clear discussion but also its biblical admonition."

Bruce A. Ware, T. Rupert and Lucille Coleman Professor of Christian Theology, The Southern Baptist Theological Seminary

"Naselli and Crowley have provided us with a practical, biblical work that cleans out the clutter in the closets of our consciences. There is gospel-centered perspective here that can bring about greater healing in our relationships, holiness in our lives, unity in our churches, and joy in our mission."

Tim Keesee, Founder and Executive Director, Frontline Missions International; author, *Dispatches from the Front*

"In his kindness God has created each of us with a conscience to bear witness to his supreme authority. The problem for many of us is that our consciences have been subject to cultural, religious, and sinful influences that warp and distort our ability to make life choices. Naselli and Crowley have provided God's people with a tremendous tool for understanding the Scriptures as they define the conscience, describe its role, and teach us to cleanse and calibrate it according to God's authority alone. The church is indebted to these two authors for their careful scholarship and practical discussion of this most important topic."

Dan Brooks, Pastor, Heritage Bible Church, Greer, South Carolina

CONSCIENCE

What It Is, How to Train It,
and Loving Those Who Differ

ANDREW DAVID NASELLI AND J. D. CROWLEY

Foreword by D. A. Carson

WHEATON, ILLINOIS

To Kara Marie Naselli,
Gloria Grace Naselli,
and Emma Elyse Naselli,

and

to Charis Kaimilani Johansen,
Ethan James Dale Crowley,
Anna Kawainohia Pruden,
Jenna Malia Crowley,
Taylor Elliot Alden Crowley,
and Nathaniel Judson Martin Crowley,

May God grace you to maintain a good
conscience and to calibrate it wisely so that
you can love other Christians when you
differ by flexing for the sake of the gospel.

CONTENTS

ILLUSTRATIONS

TABLES

FOREWORD

As Charles Taylor reminds us in his impressive book *A Secular Age*, we live in the "age of authenticity," in which individuals feel they have the right to pursue and do whatever they want: that is what makes them "authentic." Inevitably, that stance makes one suspicious of all voices of authority that seem to tug in any direction different from what makes our lives "authentic." The source or nature of that authority does not matter: government, parents, tradition, religion, morality. Nothing trumps my right to be "authentic," which from a Christian perspective is nothing other than the siren call of the supreme idol: Self. Combine this with a strong emphasis on individualism and the stage is set for the overthrow of a great deal of what was received from the past. Ironically, the voices that call for this destruction of the past and this construction of a new reality are highly selective in their treatment of authority. If they seem set to trim my authentic living, they are antiquarian, obscurantist, old-fashioned, and doubtless bigoted; if they are busy establishing the new consensus, using all the authoritative powers of the media and the cultural imagination to approve certain stances and not others, then they are prophetic, wise, liberating, and in line with history.

Small wonder, then, that this is an age that gives little thought to the nature and functions of conscience. Conscience is easily trampled if it gets in the way of authentic living. More dangerously, conscience is malleable and is easily reshaped to conform, in substantial measure, to the dictates of our age. We crush conscience in order to toss off what now appear to be the shackles of a bygone age, and then we immediately resurrect conscience in new configurations that establish new shackles, new expectations, new legalisms, new failures, new pools of guilt. For example, by determined suppression a new generation silences the voice of conscience in many sexual matters, and teases it alive when it comes to the importance of finding out where your coffee beans were grown and what we should do to protect the most recently highlighted victim.

Christians, of course, are not exempt from these pressures. But one of the things we must do to think clearly about such matters is regain biblical perspectives on the nature, nurture, and proper functions of conscience. This short book by Andy Naselli and J. D. Crowley is designed to meet this need at a popular level. It is a pleasure and a privilege to recommend it. A proper focus on conscience, especially conscience that is shaped and strengthened by Scripture, will incite us toward holiness, teach us what to do with guilt, drive us toward the gospel, draw from us something of the joy of the Lord, help the church to be a countercultural community, and even prepare us for cross-cultural missionary work. Read this book yourself, and give a copy to your friends.

D. A. Carson

PREFACE

Buy One, Get Ten Free

Some subjects in Christianity are so fertile, so abundantly promising and useful on so many different levels, that studying them reaps a harvest far beyond expectations. It's like *buy one, get ten free*. Conscience is one of those subjects. It touches on salvation, progressive sanctification, church unity, evangelism, missions, and apologetics. Yet hardly is a topic more neglected in the Christian church:

- When was the last time you heard a sermon about conscience?
- Have you ever mentioned your clean conscience in your testimony, as Paul did?
- Did those who discipled you talk much about keeping a clean conscience?
- How many ministry books emphasize the unbreakable link, as Paul did, between getting your conscience under the lordship of Christ and achieving success in church ministry and missions?
- Did you know that a proper understanding of conscience is a key to church unity?

We've written this book to help you get to know your conscience better, to put conscience back on your daily radar. Many

Christians have neglected their conscience, quite possibly you as well. And as the two of us found, this neglect is serious, a failure to give a priceless gift from God the care it deserves. For most of our lives, we didn't spend much time thinking about our conscience. Then certain events forced us to take a closer look.

For me (J. D.), conscience started catching my attention when I came back from Cambodia on home assignment and found that I couldn't make myself step over someone else's out-stretched legs. I was at a family get-together and had just gotten up from the couch to grab a refill of chips and salsa when I found my way blocked by someone's legs propped up on the coffee table. I stopped and waited for him to do the decent thing: pull his feet off the table so I could get by. But he just sat there like an uncultured boor. Then I remembered I was in America, a country famous the world over for the Statue of Liberty, baseball, and stepping over other people's legs with impunity. So I forced myself to do That Which Must Not Be Done. In Southeast Asia, one could hardly do something more offensive.

I began to wonder about my involuntary inability simply to cross over someone's legs. It felt like a pang of conscience, yet I knew that the matter had nothing to do with moral right and wrong, just proper etiquette. How had that new rule wormed its way into my conscience without my knowing it? Should it have been in my conscience at all? What is conscience? Where did it come from? How does it work? Does it always judge correctly? Can it change? How does it change? Why did mine change? How do I take care of my conscience? How is my American conscience different from the conscience of my friends in Cambodia? And so began my quest for a deeper understanding and appreciation of this gift from God.

For me (Andy), I started thinking more deeply about how the conscience works when my wife, Jenni, and I moved from our fundamentalist context in Greenville, South Carolina (we both graduated from Bob Jones University), to a conservative evangelical context in Chicago (I attended Trinity Evangelical Divinity School). We knew godly brothers and sisters at both institutions, but two actions repeatedly grieved us: (1) people in both places often lobbed verbal grenades at one another as if they were opponents, and (2) they painted each other with a broad brush that lacked sufficient nuance. The reasons for such behaviors are many and complex.[1] But I began to realize that a key cause of the divide between these two groups of Christians has to do with the conscience.

A Modest Agenda

If you're hoping that this book will directly address a particular conscience scruple with which you've been wrestling, you'll probably be disappointed. Our purpose is not to referee controversies. Neither will you find in this slender volume an exhaustive theology of conscience (though we attempt to leave no *conscience* verse unturned).

Our modest but potentially life-changing goal is to put conscience back on your daily radar, to show from Scripture what God intended and did not intend conscience to do, and to explain how your conscience works, how to care for it, and how not to damage it. We'll show you how awareness of conscience increases church unity and strengthens evangelism and missions. We'll talk about how to get along with others whose consciences enable them to hold different personal standards. And we'll give you principles for how to calibrate your conscience to better conform to God's will. We'll even include a chapter on how missionaries and other cross-cultural servants

---

[1] See Andrew David Naselli and Collin Hansen, eds., *Four Views on the Spectrum of Evangelicalism*, Counterpoints: Bible and Theology (Grand Rapids, MI: Zondervan, 2011).

can avoid pitfalls that arise from misunderstandings over differing consciences across cultures.

We believe you'll benefit greatly from studying the conscience if

- you want to know how conscience relates to your spiritual maturity;
- you want to know how to get along with people who have different personal standards than you;
- you're a pastor who suspects that a significant number of your church's problems stem from disagreements about disputable issues of conscience;
- you're a missionary who needs help negotiating the minefield of differences between missionary and local consciences and who wants to avoid importing merely cultural Christianity;
- you want to help people in your church understand why they have culture clashes with those of different opinions and habits;
- you want to learn how to adjust your conscience to match God's standards without sinning against your conscience; or
- you feel the weight of a guilty conscience and want to experience the freedom and sheer happiness of a clear, cleansed conscience.

There's a misperception that conscience-related controversies occur only in strict churches. But really all of us are incurably judgmental. As creatures made in the image of a moral God, we are incapable of *not* making moral judgments, whatever our situation. A church that thinks it has gotten beyond last generation's debates over music and wine will find that this generation's debates over recycling and child discipline are just as divisive. A believer who has prided himself on being generous on disputable matters will suddenly find himself judging a fellow believer who doesn't buy fair-trade coffee. Conscience issues will remain an important part of your personal life, your church life, and your ministry life for the rest of your life. Take a moment to think about these questions:

- What exactly is the conscience?
- What should you do when your conscience condemns you?
- How should you calibrate or adjust your conscience?
- How should you relate to fellow Christians when your consciences disagree?
- How should you relate to people in other cultures when your consciences disagree?

If you can't answer these questions, then you might be

- living under a perpetual weight of guilt;
- sinning against God by ignoring or disregarding your conscience;
- missing out on the joy that attention to conscience can provide;
- hesitating to adjust your conscience because you don't know how to do it safely;
- harming fellow Christians who hold different convictions than you;
- contributing to sinful divisiveness within Christ's church; or
- proceeding unwisely in the way you're spreading the gospel to non-Christians in other cultures.

This book addresses these issues in three steps:

1. Chapters 1–2 describe what conscience is.
2. Chapters 3–4 talk about how you should deal with your own conscience.

3. Chapters 5–6 explain how you should relate to other people when your consciences disagree.

We wrote this book because we feel so deeply that people today need clear and accurate answers to these questions. Not only do people *need* them; they *want* them. We've had many opportunities to preach, teach, and counsel about the conscience in many different venues to many different kinds of Christians, and in our experience, people love to learn about the conscience because it helps them practically.

We pray that God will use this book to educate you in how to handle your conscience for his eternal glory and your eternal good.

Christian, meet Conscience.

1

WHAT IS CONSCIENCE?

Most people probably think of the conscience as the "shoulder angel." Comic strips and films often depict an angel dressed in white on a person's right shoulder and a demon dressed in red and holding a pitchfork on the person's left shoulder (see figure 1). The angel represents the person's conscience, and the demon represents temptation. The angel attempts to persuade the person to do right, and the demon tempts the person to do wrong.

Figure 1. Shoulder angel vs. shoulder demon

This picture resonates with people because we commonly experience internal conflicts that seem like voices in our heads arguing about what to do in a particular situation. What is right? What is wrong? Thankfully, we're not left to popular perception in regard to conscience. We have the Bible to teach us what conscience is and is not. In chapter 2 we'll attempt to define conscience from the Bible. But first we want to lay out some introductory principles about conscience, principles that we'll unpack throughout the rest of the book. Most of them are pretty obvious, but it's possible that you haven't thought much about them.

Conscience Is a Human Capacity

To be human is to have a conscience. Animals don't have a conscience, even if they often seem to. I (J. D.) have a dog, Lucy, whose tail is almost permanently fixed between her legs, her eyes always averted, always guilty. We think she was mistreated as a puppy. But in spite of all appearances, Lucy doesn't have a conscience—not even the trace of one. She doesn't have a conscience because she doesn't have the capacity for moral judgment. Our cat doesn't have a conscience either, but you already knew that.

Notice we said conscience is a *capacity*. Like other human capacities such as speech and reason, it's possible for a person never to actualize or achieve the capacity of conscience. A child dies in infancy, having never spoken a single word or felt a single pang of conscience. Another child is born without the mental capacity to make moral judgments. Others, through stroke, accident, or dementia, lose the moral judgment they once had and the conscience that went with it. Still, to be human is to have the *capacity* for conscience, whether or not one is able to exercise that capacity.

Conscience Reflects the Moral Aspect of God's Image

It shouldn't surprise you that you have a conscience. You're made in the image of God, and God is a moral God, so you must be a moral creature who makes moral judgments. And what is conscience if not shining the spotlight of your moral judgment back on yourself, your thoughts, and your actions. A moral being would expect to make moral self-judgments.

So conscience is inherent in personhood. It is not the result of sin. It is not something that Christians will lose after God glorifies them. This means that Jesus, who is fully human, has a conscience. Unlike our consciences, though, Jesus's conscience perfectly matches God's will, and he has never sinned against it.

Conscience Feels Independent

But what ought to surprise you is that you would even care about the verdict of your conscience. Yet you do care, intensely. Many have taken their lives because of a secret guilt—a sin that no one else knew except that impossible-to-suppress voice within. Others have gone mad from the telltale heartbeat of a guilty conscience.

But when you think about it, why should you care what your conscience says about you? If you heard that a judge accused of a crime had decided to hear his own case, you'd laugh. First he sits on the bench and reads the charges. Then he jumps down to the witness stand to defend himself and then jumps back up to the bench to pronounce himself "not guilty." What a joke! And yet you judge yourself every day, and it doesn't feel like a joke. It's deadly serious. Why?

The *why* is a great mystery. No one knows why the conscience feels so much like an independent third party, but it probably has something to do with the relationship between two universal realities that Paul discusses in Romans chapters 1 and 2. Romans 1:19–20 claims that all humans know intuitively by the witness of nature that God exists and must be absolutely powerful. Romans 2:14–15 goes on to teach that everyone also has a conscience, an imperfect-but-accurate-enough version of God's will, as standard equipment in their hearts. Then verse 16 makes a link between the conscience and the day of judgment. Listen to these two passages side by side:

> For what can be known about God is plain to them, because God has shown it to them. For his invisible attributes, namely, his eternal power and divine nature, have been clearly perceived, ever since the creation of the world, in the things that have been made. (Rom. 1:19–20)

> For when Gentiles, who do not have the law, by nature do what the law requires, they are a law to themselves, even though they do not have the law. They show that the work of the law is written on their hearts, while their conscience also bears witness, and their conflicting thoughts accuse or even excuse them on that day when, according to my gospel, God judges the secrets of men by Christ Jesus. (Rom. 2:14–16)

Put together, these passages seem to explain conscience like this: though we all have a sense that what's going on in our conscience is secret, we also have a sense that an all-powerful, all-knowing God is in on the secret and will someday judge those secrets at his great and terrifying tribunal. We're not saying that people actually reason it out like a syllogism but that all of us intuit very strongly our accountability to an all-powerful, all-knowing God, even if we suppress that intuition, as Romans 1:18 claims. Perhaps that is why the voice of conscience seems so much like an independent judge rather than a kangaroo court.

Conscience Is a Priceless Gift from God

The conscience is a gift for your good and joy, and it is something that God—not your mother or father or anyone else—gave you.

Consider your sense of touch. That sense is a gift from God that can function as a warning system to save you from great harm. If the tip of your finger lightly brushes the top of a hot stove, your nervous system reflexively compels you to pull back your hand to avoid more pain and harm. Similarly, the guilt that your conscience makes you feel should lead you to turn from your sin to Jesus. God gave you that sense of guilt for your good.

The conscience is also a gift from God for your joy: "*Blessed is the one who has no reason to pass judgment on himself for what he approves*" (Rom. 14:22b). Like everyone else, you long to be "blessed" or happy. That's how God wired you. The ultimate way to nourish this longing is to satisfy it with the deepest and most enduring happiness, God himself, and then share that deep joy with others by loving them. Your chief end is to glorify God *by* enjoying him forever.[1] You can intensify that satisfying pursuit if you understand that your conscience is a priceless gift from God, learn how it works, and then cultivate it so that you can love others.

Conscience Wants to Be an On-Off Switch, Not a Dimmer

Conscience is all about right or wrong, black or white. It doesn't do gray scale very well. It doesn't nuance. It doesn't say, "It's complicated." It leads your thoughts to either "accuse

---

[1] We are paraphrasing John Piper's definition of what he calls "Christian hedonism." See especially John Piper, *Desiring God: Meditations of a Christian Hedonist*, 3rd ed. (Sisters, OR: Multnomah, 2003), 28.

or even excuse" (Rom. 2:15), to pronounce guilt or innocence. Because conscience wants to make such stark pronouncements, it is of utmost importance that you align your personal conscience standards with what God considers right and wrong, not just with human opinion. Otherwise, your conscience will pronounce guilty verdicts on matters of mere opinion.

Your Conscience Is for You and You Only

Conscience is personal. It is *your* conscience.[2] It is intended for you and not for someone else. And the conscience of others belongs to them and not you. You cannot, must not, force others to adopt your conscience standards. MYOC. Mind your own conscience. Accepting this one principle would solve a large percentage of relationship problems inside and outside the church. (More on this in chapter 5.)

No Two People Have Exactly the Same Conscience

If everyone had the same conscience standards, we wouldn't need passages like Romans 14 and 1 Corinthians 8, which teach people with differing consciences how to get along in their church. Let's use the triangles in figure 2 to compare the consciences of two Christians, Anne and Bill.[3] The letters in the triangles stand for various rules of right and wrong. Though not identical, Anne and Bill's consciences overlap significantly in what they view as right and wrong (C, D, E, F, and dozens of other rules). In fact, people usually agree much more in matters of conscience than they disagree.

---

[2] Gary T. Meadors defines *conscience* as "an aspect of self-awareness that produces the pain and/or pleasure we 'feel' as we reflect on the norms and values we recognize and apply. Conscience is not an outside voice. It is an inward capacity humans possess to critique themselves because the Creator provided this process as a means of moral restraint for his creation." "Conscience," in *Evangelical Dictionary of Biblical Theology*, ed. Walter A. Elwell (Grand Rapids, MI: Baker, 1996), 115.

[3] The triangles on conscience in this section are adapted from Bob Priest. See especially Robert J. Priest, "Missionary Elenctics: Conscience and Culture," *Missiology: An International Review* 22, no. 3 (1994): 291–315.

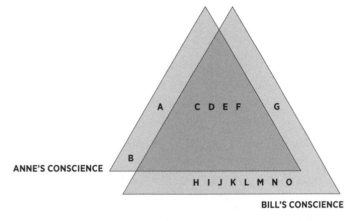

Figure 2. Two consciences

Notice, however, that Bill's conscience has more rules than Anne's (rules G, H, I, J, K, L, M, N, O). Anne sees Bill assiduously following these unnecessary rules, such as staying away from movie theaters and never playing video games, and she rolls her eyes at such "legalism." All the while, Bill is shocked that Anne can ignore these "obvious" commandments and still call herself a Christian. But Bill isn't the only one being self-righteous. Anne sees that Bill is completely oblivious to rule B and says to another friend, "Do you know that Bill buys non-fair-trade coffee? Doesn't he care about downtrodden workers in South America?" Differences in conscience cause a significant percentage of conflicts in any church.

No One's Conscience Perfectly Matches God's Will

Of course, we all tend to assume that our own conscience standards line up with God's will. Returning to our example of Anne and Bill, figure 3 superimposes God's righteous will over their consciences.

It turns out that neither Anne's nor Bill's conscience perfectly

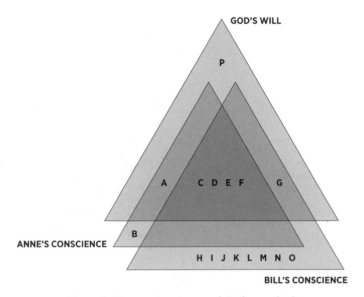

Figure 3. Human conscience and God's standards

matches God's will. No person's conscience does. Let this truth sink deep into your heart.

Anne needs to realize that buying non-fair-trade coffee (rule B) turns out *not* to be a sin before God, and Bill needs to understand that rules H, I, J, K, L, M, N, and O—including going to the theater and playing video games—are not inherent sins in God's sight. However, Anne better be thinking a whole lot more about rule G since God cares about it. And notice that Bill is wrong to omit rule A from his conscience. And they're both off about P, which doesn't show up on either of their radars. But God thinks it should!

As we come to understand God's revealed will more and more, we will have opportunities to add rules to our conscience that God's Word clearly teaches and weed out rules that God's Word treats as optional. This will take a lifetime, but we have the Spirit of God, the Word of God, and the church of God to help us.

How can you discern between your conscience and the Holy Spirit? You can't know infallibly. But you can know when it is *not* the Holy Spirit: if the message contradicts Scripture, then it is not from the Holy Spirit but from your wrongly calibrated conscience. But when the message is consistent with Scripture, the Holy Spirit is likely working *through* your conscience.

(Of course, as long as Bill considers H, I, J, K, etc. to be truly wrong actions for him, he'll need to obey his conscience in those areas, even if Scripture is silent. Say, for example, that rule H is "Don't use unfiltered Internet." As long as Bill believes God morally requires this rule for him, he must follow it. But as he understands more about conscience, he will see that he can't force Anne to agree that God has made this rule a hard-and-fast commandment for all believers. Eventually, Bill will see that rule H is not truly a commandment from God at all but an issue of wisdom.)

You Can Damage Your Conscience

You can damage the gift of conscience, just as you can damage other gifts from God. Oddly enough, you can damage it in two opposite ways: by making it insensitive and by making it oversensitive.

We make conscience *insensitive* by developing a habit of ignoring its voice of warning so that the voice gets weaker and weaker and finally disappears. Paul calls this "searing" the conscience: "Such teachings come through hypocritical liars, whose consciences have been seared as with a hot iron" (1 Tim. 4:2 NIV).

We make conscience *oversensitive* by packing it with too many rules that are actually matters of opinion, not right and wrong. Oddly enough, both kinds of damage to conscience can occur in the same person. After Paul described the conscience of false teachers as "seared," he went on to say that those same false teachers also imposed strict and unnecessary scruples about abstinence from food and marriage (1 Tim. 4:3). Jesus made the same connection between a seared conscience and an oversensitive conscience when he accused the Pharisees of scrupulously straining out gnats but then swallowing camels (Matt. 23:24), even the camel of murdering the Son of God.

This may explain why a generation ago in some parts of America, very strict churches were extremely careful about many minor issues that they perceived were right and wrong, but the same churches also trained their deacons to guard the church doors and keep out blacks. Talk about "neglect[ing] the weightier matters of the law: justice and mercy and faithfulness" (Matt. 23:23)! Talk about choking on camels!

The Two Great Principles of Conscience

Of all the principles related to conscience, two rise to the top: (1) God is the only Lord of conscience, and (2) you should always obey your conscience. These two principles come up repeatedly in this book and in your life. We'll look at the second principle first because it's the most obvious.

Principle 2: Obey It!

Even unbelievers sense deep in their hearts the importance of obeying conscience. The Bible teaches in Romans 14 and 1 Corinthians 8 that to go against your conscience when you think it's warning you correctly is *always* a sin in God's eyes. Always. Even if the action is not a sin in and of itself. Why? Because your intention is to sin. But does this mean your conscience is always correct? No. And this brings us to the first principle of conscience.

Principle 1: God Is the Only Lord of Conscience

Like the "one ring to rule them all," this conscience principle governs all the rest. Your conscience is not the lord of itself—

that's idolatry. You are not the lord of your conscience. Your parents are not the lord of your conscience (though you do well to obey them when under their care). Your pastors are not the lord of your conscience (though they care for your soul, and you would be foolish to disregard their counsel). Fellow believers are not the lord of your conscience. God is the only Lord of conscience.

This means that the second principle (obey conscience) has one critical limitation. If God, the Lord of your conscience, shows you through his Word that your conscience is registering a mistaken moral judgment and if you believe he wants you to adjust your conscience to better match his will, your conscience must bend to God. Do you remember the principle, "We must obey God rather than men" (Acts 5:29)? That holds true even when the "man" happens to be you! You must obey God rather than yourself. You must obey God rather than your conscience. If your conscience is so sacrosanct that it's off-limits even to God, that's idolatry. For example, had Peter decided to listen to his conscience instead of to God when God told him to "kill and eat!" (and, by extension, to receive Gentiles into his home), he would have committed a serious sin (Acts 10:9–16). Whenever "obey conscience!" collides with "obey God!," "obey God!" must come out on top—every time. Thankfully, a Christian with a well-calibrated conscience will rarely have to make this choice.

We promised that we would attempt to leave no *conscience* verse unturned. God is far from silent on the subject of conscience, so now it's time to look at each of the thirty occurrences of the Greek word for *conscience* in the New Testament to come up with a biblical definition.

2

HOW DO WE DEFINE CONSCIENCE
FROM THE NEW TESTAMENT?

To sort through conscience issues, we must start by defining exactly what the conscience is. People often disagree on a given topic because they are talking past each other at the basic level of definition. They are defining key terms differently. That's why it's so important to define terms when you're studying and discussing a subject. And it is best to do this at the beginning.

Defining a word is no mere language game for academics, especially when the term we are defining is in the Bible and holds significant implications for how we should live. It matters deeply, for instance, that we define *justification* as God's *declaring* us righteous rather than God's *making* us righteous. *Conscience* is one of those theological words with massive implications for how we live.

In the New Testament *conscience* translates *syneidēsis*, a word that occurs thirty times in the Greek New Testament. *Conscience* is also one of the few theologically significant New

Testament words that lacks a parallel word or group of words in the Hebrew Old Testament. But the concept of conscience is certainly in the Old Testament even if no word itself is present.[1] We will focus on the thirty times that the word *conscience* occurs in the New Testament. Then we'll draw conclusions about how to define it.

What Does the New Testament Say about the Conscience?

Our starting point is to read and reflect on all of the passages in which *conscience* (translating *syneidēsis*) appears in the New Testament. Only then can we responsibly attempt to define the word.

Conscience occurs twice in Acts, twenty times in Paul's letters, five times in Hebrews, and three times in 1 Peter. As you read all these passages, notice the words that occur along with the word *conscience*. You can learn a lot about a word by studying the words that often accompany it.

For example, imagine that you were trying to figure out what a *car door* is. You might study a sampling of one hundred sentences in which *car door* occurs, and you would probably observe that people do certain actions to a *car door*: open, shut, close, break, smash, dent, paint, scratch, and wash.

Similarly, we can learn a lot about the word *conscience* by noting the words that occur with it. We have emphasized most of those words in italics in the following survey of the thirty

---

[1] Consider these examples: (1) *Conscience* doesn't appear in Romans 14, but the concept does (and *conscience* occurs in a parallel passage in 1 Corinthians 8–10). (2) Though the word *conscience* is rare in English translations of the Old Testament, the concept isn't uncommon. *Conscience* occurs in the Old Testament one time in the ESV and NASB (1 Sam. 25:31), four times in the NIV (Gen. 20:5, 6; 1 Sam. 25:31; Job 27:6; plus "conscience-stricken" in 1 Sam. 24:5; 2 Sam. 24:10), five times in the NET (Gen. 20:5, 6; 1 Sam. 24:5; 25:31; Job 27:6), and four times in the NLT (1 Sam. 24:5; 25:31; 2 Sam. 24:10; Job 27:6). (3) *Heart* seems to be a synonym for *conscience* in passages like 1 John 3:21–22 ("Beloved, if our *heart* does not condemn us, we have confidence before God; and whatever we ask we receive from him, because we keep his commandments and do what pleases him") and Ps. 51:10a ("Create in me a clean [NIV: pure] *heart*, O God").

times that *conscience* (*syneidēsis*) appears in the New Testament. Let's look at the Book:

1. Acts 23:1. "And looking intently at the council, Paul said, 'Brothers, I have lived my life before God in all *good* conscience up to this day.'"

Paul can honestly say that he faithfully matched his actions to his understanding of God's moral standards.

2. Acts 24:16. "So I always take pains to have a *clear* conscience toward both God and man."

Paul always tries hard to make sure his actions correspond with what he believes are God's moral standards.

3. Romans 2:15. "They show that the work of the law is written on their hearts, while their conscience also *bears witness*, and their conflicting thoughts accuse or even excuse them."

Gentiles show, by obeying many of God's moral demands even though they have no access to God's revealed law (v. 14), that they have a certain consciousness of those moral standards—a consciousness that is clear enough to allow their own mind to either accuse or excuse their actions. It's even clear enough for God to use as evidence on judgment day (v. 16).

4. Romans 9:1. "I am speaking the truth in Christ—I am not lying; my conscience *bears* me *witness* in the Holy Spirit."

Paul's moral consciousness confirms through the Holy Spirit that he is not lying.

5. Romans 13:5. "Therefore one must be in subjection, not only to avoid God's wrath but also *for the sake of* conscience."

We must submit to governmental authorities, not only because they may punish us but also so that our moral consciousness won't condemn us.

6. 1 Corinthians 8:7. "However, not all possess this knowledge. But some, through former association with idols, eat food as really offered to an idol, and their conscience, being *weak*, is *defiled*."

When they eat sacrificial food, they think of it as having been sacrificed to a god and thus defile their moral consciousness, which is oversensitive because they are misinformed.

7. 1 Corinthians 8:10. "For if anyone sees you who have knowledge eating in an idol's temple, will he not *be encouraged*, if his conscience is *weak*, to eat food offered to idols?"

In the Greek text, "conscience" is the grammatical subject of the verb "encouraged" (or "strengthened" or "emboldened"). Here's a more formal translation: "For if someone sees you, the one who has knowledge, eating in an idol's temple, will not his *conscience*, being weak, *be encouraged* to eat food offered to idols?" (compare the KJV, NKJV, NASB, NET, and HCSB versions). Here's the idea: If anyone sees you, who have an informed moral consciousness on this issue (i.e., you know that there are no real gods but one), eating in an idol's temple, won't that person's misinformed moral consciousness be emboldened to sin against his own conscience by eating food sacrificed to idols?

8. 1 Corinthians 8:12. "Thus, sinning against your brothers and *wounding* their conscience when it is *weak*, you sin against Christ."

When you embolden your brothers and sisters to disregard their moral consciousness (even if it's misinformed), you are sinning against them by causing them to feel intense guilt since their misinformed (and thus oversensitive) moral consciousness condemns them. In that way, you also sin against Christ.

9–10. 1 Corinthians 10:25, 27. "Eat whatever is sold in the meat market without raising any question *on the ground of* conscience. . . . If one of the unbelievers invites you to dinner and you are disposed to go, eat whatever is set before you without raising any question *on the ground of* conscience."

You don't need to bother asking where your meat came from because it doesn't matter if it was sacrificed to idols. That is a theologically unnecessary question. Your moral consciousness should not condemn you for eating such meat.

11–13. 1 Corinthians 10:28–29. "But if someone says to you, 'This has been offered in sacrifice,' then do not eat it, for the sake of the one who informed you, and *for the sake of* conscience—I do not mean your conscience, but his. For why should my liberty *be determined by* someone else's conscience?"

You shouldn't eat meat that someone told you was sacrificed to idols if the result would be that that person's moral consciousness would condemn you for eating. Why should someone else's (misinformed) moral consciousness judge yours?

14. 2 Corinthians 1:12. "For our boast is this, the *testimony* of our conscience, that we behaved in the world with simplicity and godly sincerity, not by earthly wisdom but by the grace of God, and supremely so toward you."

Their own moral consciousness testifies that they conducted themselves in the world with integrity and godly sincerity.

15. 2 Corinthians 4:2. "But we have renounced disgraceful, underhanded ways. We refuse to practice cunning or to tamper with God's word, but by the open statement of the truth we would *commend ourselves to* everyone's conscience in the sight of God."

By plainly setting forth the truth, they appeal to each individual's moral consciousness (compare our comment on 2 Cor. 5:11, the next passage). God sees all of us as we are.

16. 2 Corinthians 5:11. "Therefore, knowing the fear of the Lord, we persuade others. But what we are is known to God, and I hope it is *known* also to your conscience."

God knows and approves of what they are, and Paul hopes that the Corinthians' moral consciousness approves of them as well. Paul is challenging the believers in Corinth to make a moral judgment about his faithfulness and validity according to their personal moral standards. Paul is confident that their conscience will use the right standards and that he will pass the test. He is essentially saying, "Test me by your conscience."

17. 1 Timothy 1:5. "The aim of our charge is love that issues from a pure heart and a *good* conscience and a sincere faith."

Paul gives a solemn charge about troublemakers hindering Timothy's ministry, and his goal in doing so is that they would return to the highest motivation and standard of all: love, which flows out of a person whose heart is pure and who thinks and acts consistently with the standards of his moral consciousness.

18. 1 Timothy 1:19. ". . . holding faith and a *good* conscience. By rejecting this, some have made shipwreck of their faith."

Timothy must never let go of his trust in God and must always live according to his moral consciousness. Some have failed to do this and have destroyed their lives. John Calvin concludes, "A bad conscience is, therefore, the mother of all heresies."[2] There is a connection between a bad conscience and apostasy; objections to Christianity are fundamentally moral, not intellectual (cf. John 3:19–20).

19. 1 Timothy 3:9. "They must hold the mystery of the faith with a *clear* conscience."

Deacons must live uprightly (v. 8) and affirm orthodox

---

[2] John Calvin, *Commentaries on the Epistles to Timothy, Titus, and Philemon*, ed. and trans. William Pringle (Edinburgh: Calvin Translation Society, 1856), 46.

theology with a pure moral consciousness. They must not deceive others about their character (v. 8) or the doctrine they actually believe. Right living and right doctrine go together (cf. 1:19).

20. 1 Timothy 4:2. ". . . through the insincerity of liars whose consciences are *seared*."

By repeatedly suppressing their moral consciousness, these hypocritical liars have desensitized their moral consciousness with the result that they feel no guilt when they teach false doctrines.

21. 2 Timothy 1:3. "I thank God whom I serve, as did my ancestors, with a *clear* conscience, as I remember you constantly in my prayers night and day."

Paul serves God in such a way that his moral consciousness approves of his work.

22. Titus 1:15. "To the pure, all things are pure, but to the defiled and unbelieving, nothing is pure; but both their minds and their consciences are *defiled*."

Because of their sins, their minds don't think rightly, and their moral consciousness doesn't function correctly.

23. Hebrews 9:9b. "According to this arrangement, gifts and sacrifices are offered that cannot *perfect* the conscience of the worshiper."

Under the old covenant, Israelites offered God gifts and sacrifices that couldn't completely clear the condemnation they felt from their moral consciousness.

24. Hebrews 9:14. ". . . how much more will the blood of Christ, who through the eternal Spirit offered himself without blemish to God, *purify* our conscience from dead works to serve the living God."

The blood of Christ clears all the condemnation we feel

from our moral consciousness. It cleanses our moral consciousness, which enables us to serve the living God.

25. Hebrews 10:2. "Otherwise, would they not have ceased to be offered, since the worshipers, having once been cleansed, would no longer *have* any consciousness of sins?"

This is one of the two times in the New Testament that *syneidēsis* means merely "consciousness" (in the sense of "awareness") rather than "moral consciousness" or "conscience." (The other is 1 Pet. 2:19.)

26. Hebrews 10:22. ". . . let us draw near with a true heart in full assurance of faith, with our hearts sprinkled clean from an *evil* conscience and our bodies washed with pure water."

We should draw close to God with a sincere heart and with the complete confidence that faith brings because Jesus has sprinkled our hearts to cleanse us from a guilty moral consciousness.

27. Hebrews 13:18. "Pray for us, for we are sure that we have a *clear* conscience, desiring to act honorably in all things."

They are sure that they are living and acting according to the high standards of their moral consciousness. They are trying to live in a way that honors God.

28. 1 Peter 2:19. "For this is a gracious thing, when, *mindful* [NIV: 'conscious'] of God, one endures sorrows while suffering unjustly."

This is the second of the two times in the New Testament that *syneidēsis* means merely "consciousness" (in the sense of "awareness") rather than "moral consciousness" or "conscience." (The other is Heb. 10:2.)

29. 1 Peter 3:16. ". . . having a *good* conscience, so that, when you are slandered, those who revile your good behavior in Christ may be put to shame."

Christians should live in such a way that their moral consciousness approves of their actions.

30. 1 Peter 3:21. "Baptism, which corresponds to this, now saves you, not as a removal of dirt from the body but as an appeal to God for a *good* conscience, through the resurrection of Jesus Christ."

God saved Noah and his family through water (v. 20). That destructive water is a "type" or pattern of Christian baptism. Baptism itself doesn't save you by washing physical filth off you; it represents that God has cleansed your guilty moral consciousness by forgiving your sins through Jesus's death, resurrection, and ascension.[3]

After carefully reading all of the above passages in which the term *conscience* occurs, you should be able to answer these two questions: What can the conscience be? And what can the conscience do?

What Can the Conscience Be?

The New Testament speaks of the conscience positively in two ways and negatively in six ways.

Positively

1. The conscience can be good in the sense of blameless, clear, clean, and pure (Acts 23:1; 24:16; 1 Tim. 1:5, 19; 3:9; 2 Tim. 1:3; Heb. 13:18; 1 Pet. 3:16, 21).
2. The conscience can be cleansed, that is, cleared, perfected, purified, washed, purged, and sprinkled clean (Heb. 9:9, 14; 10:22).

---

[3] See Wayne Grudem, *1 Peter: An Introduction and Commentary*, Tyndale New Testament Commentaries 17 (Downers Grove, IL: InterVarsity Press, 1988), 171–72; Thomas R. Schreiner, *1, 2 Peter, Jude*, New American Commentary 37 (Nashville: Broadman, 2003), 193–97.

Negatively

1. The conscience can be weak (1 Cor. 8:7, 10, 12).
2. The conscience can be wounded (1 Cor. 8:12).
3. The conscience can be defiled (1 Cor. 8:7; Titus 1:15).
4. The conscience can be encouraged or emboldened to sin (1 Cor. 8:10).
5. The conscience can be evil or guilty (Heb. 10:22).
6. The conscience can be seared as with a hot iron (1 Tim. 4:2).

We've listed these six negative descriptions in a generally declining order, from mistaken ("weak") to bad to worse. The final term in 1 Tim. 4:2 depicts a deadened conscience. John MacArthur explains,

> A weak conscience is not the same as a seared conscience. A seared conscience becomes inactive, silent, rarely accusing, insensitive to sin. But the weakened conscience usually is hypersensitive and overactive about issues that are not sins. Ironically, a weak conscience is more likely to accuse than a strong conscience. Scripture calls this a weak conscience because it is *too easily wounded*. People with weak consciences tend to fret about things that should provoke no guilt in a mature Christian who knows God's truth.[4]

What Can the Conscience Do?

In the New Testament, the conscience can do three actions.

1. The conscience can bear witness or confirm (Rom. 2:15; 9:1; 2 Cor. 1:12; 4:2; 5:11).
2. The conscience can judge or try to determine another person's freedom (1 Cor. 10:29).

---

[4] John MacArthur, *The Vanishing Conscience* (Dallas: Word, 1994), 44 (italics in the original). Cf. John R. W. Stott, *Guard the Truth: The Message of 1 Timothy and Titus*, The Bible Speaks Today (Downers Grove, IL: InterVarsity Press, 1996), 112.

3. The conscience can lead one to act a certain way. The New Testament gives four examples: it can lead you either to accuse or defend yourself based on how your conscience bears witness (Rom. 2:15); it can lead you to submit to the authorities (Rom. 13:5); it can lead you not to bother asking where your meat came from because eating meat sacrificed to idols is not something your conscience should condemn you for (1 Cor. 10:25, 27); and it can lead you not to eat meat that someone tells you was sacrificed to idols for the sake of that person's conscience (1 Cor. 10:28).[5]

So How Should We Define the Conscience?

After considering all these passages, here is our attempt to define the conscience: *The conscience is your consciousness of what you believe is right and wrong.*[6] Consciousness means awareness or sense, and we include that word in the definition to make it more memorable.

Our definition has some noteworthy implications:

1. *Conscience produces different results for people based on different moral standards.* That's why our definition says, "The conscience is your consciousness of *what you believe* is right and wrong." What you believe is right and wrong is not necessarily the same as what actually *is* right and wrong. As Justin Taylor puts it, "A clear conscience is a necessary but not a sufficient condition of innocence."[7] So someone's "clear" conscience may actually be evil because it is based on immoral standards. You might notice this, for example, when

---

[5] The final way differs from the first three because in 1 Cor. 10:28, it is not your own conscience that keeps you from eating but sensitivity to another person's conscience.

[6] Compare our definition with how the standard Greek lexicon defines *syneidēsis*: "the inward faculty that distinguishes right and wrong." Walter Bauer, Frederick William Danker, William F. Arndt, and F. Wilbur Gingrich, eds., *A Greek-English Lexicon of the New Testament and Other Early Christian Literature*, 3rd ed. (Chicago: University of Chicago Press, 2000), 967.

[7] Justin Taylor, Twitter post, April 16, 2015, https://twitter.com/between2worlds/status/5888 17466198872064.

you listen to some pro-abortion advocates talk about abortion as if it were a civil rights issue or a positive good. Their standard for determining right and wrong is immoral.[8] What moral standard should you base your conscience on? Martin Luther's famous statement nails it: "My conscience is captive to the Word of God."[9]

2. *Conscience can change.* Your conscience is your consciousness of what you believe is right and wrong *at any given point in time*, and it can change for a complex of reasons, good and bad. (We discuss this further in chapter 4.)

3. *Conscience functions as a guide, monitor, witness, and judge.* Your conscience *guides* you to help you conform to moral standards, *monitors* how you conform to them, *testifies* to how you conform to them, and *judges* you for how you conform to them, thus making you feel guilt and pain (see table 1).[10]

FUNCTION	TIME	NEGATIVE	POSITIVE
Guide	Looks forward	It warns you before you do "wrong."	It urges you to do "right."
Monitor, witness, judge	Looks backward	It accuses and condemns you when you do "wrong."	It commends and defends you when you do "right."

Table 1. The multiple functions of the conscience

The conscience is your consciousness of what you believe is right and wrong. It's basically your moral consciousness or your moral awareness turned back on yourself. A good example

---

[8] Cf. Scott Klusendorf, *The Case for Life: Equipping Christians to Engage the Culture* (Wheaton, IL: Crossway, 2009); Justin Taylor, "'Abortion Is about God': Piper's Passionate, Prophetic Pro-Life Preaching," in *For the Fame of God's Name: Essays in Honor of John Piper*, ed. Sam Storms and Justin Taylor (Wheaton, IL: Crossway, 2010), 328–50.

[9] Roland H. Bainton, *Here I Stand: A Life of Martin Luther* (New York: Abingdon-Cokesbury, 1950), 182.

[10] Cf. Richard Sibbes, *The Complete Works of Richard Sibbes, D.D.*, ed. Alexander Balloch Grosart (Edinburgh: Nichol, 1862), 1:210–11; J. I. Packer, *A Quest for Godliness: The Puritan Vision of the Christian Life* (Wheaton, IL: Crossway, 1990), 110–11.

of this is Paul in Acts 23:1: "I have lived my life before God in all good conscience up to this day." How could Paul, who persecuted so many Christians before his conversion, honestly say that? Because even when he persecuted Christians, he did it with a clear conscience. His fallible conscience was deeply wrong when he killed believers, but he didn't recognize his error until after God saved and transformed him.[11]

So What?

Now you have a better idea of what the word *conscience* means. So what? Why does it matter that you understand what the conscience is? It's crucial for answering four critical questions—questions that the next four chapters address:

- What should you do when your conscience condemns you? (ch. 3)
- How should you calibrate your conscience to match God's will? (ch. 4)
- How should you relate to fellow Christians when your consciences disagree? (ch. 5)
- How should you relate to people in other cultures when your consciences disagree? (ch. 6)

---

[11] See James Montgomery Boice, *Acts: An Expositional Commentary* (Grand Rapids, MI: Baker, 1997), 375. Alternatively, in Acts 23:1 Paul may be referring to his clear conscience regarding his conduct since becoming a Christian; see I. Howard Marshall, *Acts: An Introduction and Commentary*, Tyndale New Testament Commentaries 5 (Downers Grove, IL: InterVarsity Press, 1980), 382; David G. Peterson, *The Acts of the Apostles*, Pillar New Testament Commentary (Grand Rapids, MI: Eerdmans, 2009), 612–13.

3

WHAT SHOULD YOU DO WHEN YOUR CONSCIENCE CONDEMNS YOU?

All of us know the misery of having our conscience accuse us and condemn us and make us feel guilty. It's a horrible feeling. What should you do when this happens?

John MacArthur observes, "The conscience may be the most underappreciated and least understood attribute of humanity. Psychology . . . is usually less concerned with understanding the conscience than with attempting to silence it."[1] Some people devise ways to soothe their conscience or ignore it or stretch it so that they don't feel guilty. That's foolish. Your conscience is a gift. God gave it to you for your good. And when it's condemning you, you need to discern why and then respond.

If you rightly understand how holy God is and how sinful you are, your conscience will rightly condemn you when you

[1] John MacArthur, *The Vanishing Conscience* (Dallas: Word, 1994), 50.

sin against God. Like everyone else, you fall short of the glory of God, and your conscience monitors your sins and testifies in ugly detail when you have sinned. Your guilty conscience is a barrier between you and God. This can make you despair. Or it can lead to passionate praise.

The Bible proclaims good news of a clean conscience for both the lost and the saved.

A Clean Conscience for the Lost

As you can imagine, the promise of a life with a clean conscience before God is a powerful attraction for the lost to come to Christ. We know of no other religion that freely offers such comprehensive and eternal cleansing at the deepest level of conscience. "Your sins are forgiven," Jesus pronounced (Matt. 9:2). "How much more will the blood of Christ, who through the eternal Spirit offered himself without blemish to God, purify our conscience from dead works to serve the living God" (Heb. 9:14). When we share the gospel with non-Christians, we should stress this incredible promise of a clean conscience.

I (J. D.) live in Cambodia among people who are burdened with unimaginable guilt. Some of them murdered dozens, even hundreds, during the horrible Khmer Rouge period. Others would have murdered their tormentors if they had had a chance. Many of them have killed their babies through abortion. Millions have committed sexual sins. Tens of thousands of men have been unfaithful to their wives and then brought AIDS and other diseases home to infect their wives and babies. Many have broken apart families through their immorality and adultery. They've stolen many things and defrauded the poor of property and land. They've taken advantage of the weak and looked down on minorities and aliens. They've hated people and wished death on them, even hiring sorcerers to harm them.

Worst of all, they've run headlong into the worship of idols and demons and houses and cars and money instead of the true and living God. What can we say to people who carry with them such terrible secrets and unbearable burdens? What word of hope do we have?

This word: God so loved the world that he gave his one and only Son to redeem all who trust in Christ. God forgives and covers all their sin, and he *never counts that sin against them for all eternity* because he counted that sin against Christ instead. Only this message can comfort a non-Christian's guilt-racked conscience.

The Supercharged Conscience of a Christian

But once you come to Christ and receive that cleansing of conscience, does conscience now fall silent? Quite the opposite! Christians are surprised and sometimes discouraged to find that the condemnations of conscience are even stronger after becoming a child of God. Perhaps you, too, have had thoughts like this: "If I'm making progress toward holiness with the help of the Holy Spirit, why do I keep feeling like I'm a worse sinner than before? Becoming a Christian was supposed to relieve my conscience. What's going on?"

We shouldn't be surprised when this happens. The moment God accepts you as his child, he gives you the greatest gift he could ever give a child of God: his Holy Spirit to dwell in you. The Holy Spirit comes in to encourage you, comfort you, and be your dearest friend. But he also comes in to reveal to you any sin that is robbing you of joy and to lead you into mortal combat against that sin (Rom. 8:13–14).

When the Holy Spirit comes in, he supercharges your consciousness of sin by writing his laws on your heart (Jer. 31:33–34). He opens your eyes to see sins that you didn't even know were sins, like pride, greed, and covetousness. He reveals to you all the little idols in your heart's idol factory. As you read the Bible every day, you see more and more how good and holy God is and how filthy you are.

Don't expect this struggle to get any easier as you mature in your faith. The war against indwelling sin grows only stronger. This is because your knowledge about God's will in the Scriptures usually increases at a faster pace than you can put that knowledge into practice. And that gap between knowledge and obedience grows as the years go on (see figure 4).

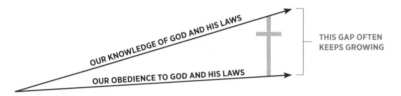

Figure 4. Consciousness of truth often grows
faster than obedience to truth

There is generally a proportional relationship between how mature you are as a Christian and how aware you are of your sinfulness. The more you grow by means of grace, the more sensitive you become to your sinfulness. Paul himself increasingly realized his sinfulness: he referred to himself as "the least of the apostles" (1 Cor. 15:9), then "the very least of all the saints" (Eph. 3:8), and finally, the "foremost" of "sinners" (1 Tim. 1:15). Like Paul, you are growing in holiness every day. But you may not feel like it! You're a saint and a sinner at the same time.

That explains *why* a Christian often feels so wretched. But then what? If the gap between what we should be and what we really are keeps growing, how can we possibly escape complete despair in the Christian life? What do we do with this supercharged knowledge of God and this supercharged conscience with its supercharged condemnations?

A Clean Conscience for the Saved

Only an ever-increasing trust in Christ's work on the cross can fill this ever-widening gap and keep us from despair. God's solution for us to have a clean conscience throughout our lives is simple and profound: "If we confess our sins, he is faithful and just to forgive us our sins and to cleanse us from all unrighteousness" (1 John 1:9). The sentences before and after this solution capture the world's solutions for a defiled conscience, namely, *to deny* that we have any sin at all and *to defend* our sin (vv. 8, 10). These solutions are still popular today in secular counseling.

But notice something surprising about the wording of 1 John 1:9. You expect John to say, "If we confess our sins, God is *kind and merciful*." Instead he says, "faithful and just." If you've just confessed to a crime, the last thing you want to hear is that the judge assigned to your case is the most just and righteous judge in the city. No, you want to hear that he is the most *merciful* judge. But John deliberately chooses two words that are completely counterintuitive. In these two words lies the Christian's secret for a cleansed and peaceful conscience. The reason for John's unusual choice of words becomes clear when you read ahead just a couple sentences: "My little children, I am writing these things to you so that you may not sin. But if anyone does sin, we have an advocate with the Father, Jesus Christ the righteous. He is the *propitiation* for our sins, and not for ours only but also for the sins of the whole world" (1 John 2:1–2).

Propitiation is a sacrifice that turns aside the justly deserved wrath of God and completely satisfies all of his righteous demands for justice. Christian, Christ is your propitiation. He has already turned aside God's wrath against you by absorbing all of it into himself on the cross. If you, then, as a Christian commit a sin (which you do every day) and repentantly confess that sin to God, God would be *un*faithful and *un*just to refuse to forgive you. God not only promises to forgive you but also promises to *cleanse* you! So when your conscience condemns you, go boldly before God's throne of grace so that you may find mercy and grace (cf. Heb. 4:16).

> What can wash away my sin?
> Nothing but the blood of Jesus.
> What can make me whole again?
> Nothing but the blood of Jesus.[2]

That's true for your conscience. What can purify your conscience? Nothing but the blood of Jesus. Jesus's blood will purify or cleanse your conscience from acts that lead to death so that you may serve the living God (Heb. 9:14).

> There is a fountain fill'd with blood,
> Drawn from Emmanuel's veins;
> And sinners plung'd beneath that flood,
> Lose *all their guilty stains*.[3]

When Conscience Tempts You to Despair

At times you may fail so miserably that your condemning conscience tempts you to despair of all hope that you could ever draw near to God. But we can draw near to God with a sincere heart and with the full assurance that faith brings "*because* we have had our hearts sprinkled clean from an evil conscience and our bodies washed in pure water" (Heb. 10:22 NET). God's Word repeatedly promises that Jesus can cleanse your conscience so that you can draw near to God.

---

[2] Robert Lowry, "Nothing but the Blood of Jesus," in *Gospel Music*, by W. Howard Doane and Robert Lowry (New York: Biglow & Main, 1876).

[3] William Cowper, "There Is a Fountain," in *A Collection of Psalms and Hymns, from Various Authors: For the Use of Serious and Devout Christians of All Denominations* (London: Clement Watts, 1772), 187 (italics added).

We live at a special time in the history of redemption. God's people can now have a clear conscience because Jesus inaugurated the new covenant through his life, death, and resurrection. In former times, God's people under the old covenant had guilty consciences that hindered how they approached God. The gifts and sacrifices that God's people offered could not perfect or clear the conscience of the worshiper (Heb. 9:9). But now we can confidently approach God on the basis of Jesus's definitive conscience-cleansing work on the cross. Now we can have a "clear conscience" (Heb. 13:18).[4]

Only the cross can fill that ever-widening gap between your consciousness of what you ought to be and your actual obedience. As you mature in your faith, you grow increasingly in love with Christ and his gospel; you place your trust more and more in Christ to make you acceptable before God; and you wait with greater and greater anticipation for the day when Christ will come back and make your obedience match your knowledge.

"All this is true, and much more"

In one scene of John Bunyan's *The Pilgrim's Progress*, Christian faces off with Apollyon. After Apollyon accurately accuses Christian of a series of sins, Christian basically replies, "You're right. But I'm actually even worse than that." That disarming statement sets up the deathblow:

> Apollyon accused, "You almost fainted when you first set out, when you almost choked in the Swamp of Despond. You also attempted to get rid of your burden in the wrong way, instead of patiently waiting for the Prince to take it off. You sinfully slept and lost your scroll, you were almost

---

[4] See Peter T. O'Brien, *The Letter to the Hebrews*, Pillar New Testament Commentary (Grand Rapids, MI: Eerdmans, 2010), 367.

persuaded to go back at the sight of the lions, and when you talk of your journey and of what you have heard and seen, you inwardly desire your own glory in all you do and say."

"All this is true, and much more that you have failed to mention," Christian agreed. "But the Prince whom I now serve and honor is merciful and ready to forgive. Besides, these infirmities possessed me while I was in your country, for there I allowed them to come in. But I have groaned under them, have been sorry for them, and have obtained pardon from my Prince."[5]

This passage echoes what Bunyan writes in *The Jerusalem Sinner Saved*:

Satan is loath to part with a great sinner. What, my true servant, quoth he, my old servant, wilt thou forsake me now? Having so often sold thyself to me to work wickedness, wilt thou forsake me now? Thou horrible wretch, dost not know, that thou has sinned thyself beyond the reach of grace, and dost thou think to find mercy now? Art not thou a murderer, a thief, a harlot, a witch, a sinner of the greatest size, and dost thou look for mercy now? Dost thou think that Christ will foul his fingers with thee? It is enough to make angels *blush*, saith Satan, to see so vile a one knock at heaven-gates for mercy, and wilt thou be so abominably bold to do it? Thus Satan dealt with me, says the great sinner, when at first I came to Jesus Christ. And what did you reply? saith the tempted. Why, I granted the whole charge to be true, says the other. And what, did you despair, or how? No, saith he, I said, I am Magdalene, I am Zaccheus, I am the thief, I am the harlot, I am the publican, I am the prodigal, and one of Christ's murderers; yea, worse than any of these, and yet God was so far off from rejecting of

[5] John Bunyan, *The Pilgrim's Progress: From This World to That Which Is to Come*, ed. C. J. Lovik (Wheaton, IL: Crossway, 2009), 89–90.

me (as I found afterwards) that there was music and dancing in his house for me, and for joy that I was come home unto him.[6]

These exchanges remind us of the hymn "Before the Throne of God Above," which includes a line where we could swap the word "Satan" with "conscience":

When Satan [conscience] tempts me to despair
And tells me of the guilt within,
Upward I look and see him there
Who made an end of all my sin.
Because the sinless Savior died,
My sinful soul is counted free,
For God, the Just, is satisfied
To look on him and pardon me.[7]

And here's another one:

What, tho' the accuser [our conscience] roar
Of ills that we have done!
We know them all, and thousands more,
Jehovah findeth none.[8]

When your conscience rightly condemns you, you should confess your sins to God and any other person you've sinned against in order to make things right. And instead of wallowing in self-pity about how wretched you are, look to Jesus. Look to the cross. Jesus lived, died, and rose again for sinners like you, and God will save you if you turn from your sins and trust Jesus.

---

[6] John Bunyan, *The Jerusalem Sinner Saved* (Edinburgh: Religious Tract Society, 1829), 42–43.
[7] Written in 1863 by Charitie Lees Smith (later Bancroft, then de Chenez), 1841–1923. John Julian, ed., *A Dictionary of Hymnology* (New York: Charles Scribner's Sons, 1892), 109.
[8] Samuel Whitelock Gandy, "What Tho' the Accuser Roar," in *Hymns for the Poor of the Flock* (London: Central Tract Depot, 1841), 43.

That's the gospel. There's no better news than that when your conscience is rightly condemning you.

————

Thank you, Father, for the power of the cross. Thank you that Jesus lived, died, and rose again for sinners like me. Thank you for promising to save me from my sins and cleanse my evil conscience if I turn from my sins and trust Jesus. Because the sinless Savior died, my sinful soul is counted free, for you, the Just, are satisfied to look on him and pardon me. Amen.

4

HOW SHOULD YOU CALIBRATE YOUR CONSCIENCE?

The previous chapter addresses what to do when your conscience *rightly* condemns you. But can your conscience *wrongly* condemn you? Can it *wrongly* guide you? What should you do if your conscience isn't functioning accurately?

———

Are you prepared to maintain a good conscience even if it will cost you your job? What if your boss wants you to manipulate the finances so that he can take cash that does not belong to him?

Are you prepared to maintain a good conscience even if it will cost you your business? What if your government requires you to provide health care for your employees that includes paying for abortion-causing contraception?[1]

---

[1] This was the case for Hobby Lobby. Fortunately, the US Supreme Court ruled in their favor on June 30, 2014.

Are you prepared to maintain a good conscience even if it means you'll go to jail? What if your government declares that affirming what God's Word says about marriage and sex is "hate speech" and that offenders will go to prison? What if your government requires you to affirm that it is good for a man to marry a man or a woman to marry a woman? What if officials enforce a law that Christian institutions (such as a church or college) must be willing to hire pastors or professors who are "married" to another person of the same gender or else face discrimination charges?

Martin Luther believed that maintaining a good conscience was worth going to prison for and even dying for. That great Reformer discovered in the Bible that God justifies sinners by grace alone through faith alone in Christ alone. The Roman Catholic Church excommunicated Luther and demanded that he recant his writings, but at Luther's hearing before the Diet of Worms, he refused to go against his conscience, even if it meant death: "Unless I am convicted by Scripture and plain reason—I do not accept the authority of popes and councils, for they have contradicted each other—*my conscience is captive to the Word of God*. I cannot and I will not recant anything, for *to go against conscience is neither right nor safe*. God help me. Amen."[2]

Luther offers a timeless principle: You should maintain a good conscience even if it means you'll suffer prison or death. It's that important.

And that's why it's so important that you learn how your conscience works and how you may need to adjust it. It would be a shame to go to prison or die because you held a conviction based on a *misinformed* conscience. In this chapter, we'll explore the important role your conscience plays in your daily

---

[2] Roland H. Bainton, *Here I Stand: A Life of Martin Luther* (New York: Abingdon-Cokesbury, 1950), 182 (italics added).

choices and consider what to do when it *wrongly* condemns you or isn't functioning accurately.

Should You Listen to Your Conscience?

Understanding what the conscience is and how it works should encourage you to maintain a good conscience. It should scare you to think of the consequences of sinning against your conscience. You don't want to travel the pathway from a weak conscience to one that is wounded and defiled and emboldened to sin, then to an evil conscience, and finally to one seared as with a hot iron.

John MacArthur recounts a tragedy that powerfully illustrates the dangers of ignoring the conscience:

> In 1984 an Avianca Airlines jet crashed in Spain. Investigators studying the accident made an eerie discovery. The "black box" cockpit recorders revealed that several minutes before impact a shrill, computer-synthesized voice from the plane's automatic warning system told the crew repeatedly in English, "Pull up! Pull up!"
>
> The pilot, evidently thinking the system was malfunctioning, snapped, "Shut up, Gringo!" and switched the system off. Minutes later the plane plowed into the side of a mountain. Everyone on board died.
>
> When I saw that tragic story on the news shortly after it happened, it struck me as a perfect parable of the way modern people treat the warning messages of their consciences.
>
> . . . The wisdom of our age says guilt feelings are nearly always erroneous or hurtful; therefore we should switch them off. . . .
>
> The conscience is generally seen by the modern world as a defect that robs people of their self-esteem. Far from being a defect or a disorder, however, our ability to sense our own guilt is a tremendous gift from God. He designed

the conscience into the very framework of the human soul. It is the automatic warning system that tells us, "Pull up! Pull up!" before we crash and burn.[3]

MacArthur goes on to describe how we build up resistance to our conscience gradually:

> Our conscience is like the nerve endings in our fingertips. Its sensitivity to external stimuli can be damaged by the buildup of callouses or even wounded so badly as to be virtually impervious to any feeling. Paul also wrote of the dangers of a calloused conscience (1 Cor. 8:10), a wounded conscience (v. 12), and a seared conscience (1 Tim. 4:2).[4]

How do we avoid a calloused conscience? "The way to keep the conscience tender," writes Jonathan Edwards, "is to the utmost to resist sin."[5]

Perhaps you have been deceiving other people. Perhaps you have cheated in your college coursework. Perhaps you are lying to your accountability partners about how you're really doing. Perhaps you're defrauding your employer or employees or customers in some way. Perhaps you are being unfaithful to your spouse. There are a multitude of ways you might be triggering your conscience to rightly condemn you.

When you sin, your conscience should be screaming at you to get right with God. Should you ignore your conscience or try to rationalize away your sinful behavior as trivial? No. Listen to your conscience. Cultivate a good conscience.

I (J. D.) drive a Toyota RAV4, and its warning light is perpetually on and perpetually ignored. The computer says it's the

---

[3] John MacArthur, *The Vanishing Conscience* (Dallas: Word, 1994), 36.
[4] Ibid., 39.
[5] Jonathan Edwards, "Conviction and the Uses of Order," in *Works of Jonathan Edwards*, vol. 19, *Sermons and Discourses, 1734–1738*, ed. M. X. Lesser (New Haven, CT: Yale University Press, 2001), 270. Cf. Wayne Grudem, *1 Peter: An Introduction and Commentary*, Tyndale New Testament Commentaries 17 (Downers Grove, IL: InterVarsity Press, 1988), 161.

catalytic converter, an unnecessary component in Cambodia, which has no pollution laws. But what if something occurred subtly in the vehicle that had the potential to reap catastrophe? I'm so used to ignoring the light that I would never notice it and would do nothing. Ignoring the warning lights of conscience can put us in the same dangerous position, which is why it's best to address the issues of conscience directly, not hope they just go away.

In fact, that pathway leads to the most satisfying experience in this world. As one New Testament scholar observes, "The possession of a good conscience is 'the best pillow' for enjoying a peaceful Christian life."[6] We want a conscience that is good, blameless, clear, clean, and pure.

So you should listen to your conscience. But should you *always* do what it says, without exception?

How Reliable Is Your Conscience?

The principle of Romans 14:22b–23 is so simple, yet we need God's grace to follow it: "Blessed is the one who has no reason to pass judgment on himself for what he approves. But whoever has doubts is condemned if he eats, because the eating is not from faith. For *whatever does not proceed from faith is sin*." The principle is this: Don't sin against your conscience. Listen to your conscience. Cultivate a good conscience. Luther was right: "to go against conscience is neither right nor safe."[7]

But is your conscience perfectly reliable? As we've already stated, no one's conscience perfectly matches God's will in this life. Nevertheless, we believe that you should *generally* always follow your conscience. "Generally always"? Yes, that's the general rule, so that's what we should emphasize. God didn't

---

[6] I. Howard Marshall, *A Critical and Exegetical Commentary on the Pastoral Epistles*, International Critical Commentary (London: T&T Clark, 1999), 219.
[7] Bainton, *Here I Stand*, 182.

give you a conscience so that you would disregard it or distrust it. Romans 14:22b–23 teaches that a person who lives according to their conscience is "blessed." So the general principle, especially for Christians who have the Holy Spirit and the holy Scripture, is that you should listen to and obey your conscience.

We emphasize this because some recent treatments talk about the conscience as if it were a hopelessly faulty instrument that functions unreliably.[8] We don't want to give that impression. What good is an unreliable instrument? As a general rule, you should assume that your conscience is reliable, even if it isn't perfect. And since conscience is usually right, the Bible says that we should do what our conscience says until we are convinced from Scripture that it needs adjusting.

But calling this a *general* rule means that there are exceptions. The exceptions in this case matter significantly in our lives.

Should we follow the popular advice in Walt Disney's 1940 animated film *Pinocchio*? After the Blue Fairy appoints Jiminy Cricket as Pinocchio's official conscience, these are her parting words: "Now remember, Pinocchio, be a good boy, and always let your conscience be your guide." Jiminy Cricket then sings those words to Pinocchio with a catchy tune: "Always let your conscience be your guide."

Always?

Ed Clowney wisely observes, "The Walt Disney version of Pinocchio has given us the cartoon image of conscience as a friendly cricket, an effort, perhaps, to reduce the hostility with which people are inclined to view the promptings of conscience.

---

[8] For example, Christopher Ash, in *Pure Joy: Rediscover Your Conscience* (Nottingham, UK: Inter-Varsity Press, 2012), titles his second chapter "The unreliable voice" (30–41). We think that "unreliable" is not the best word for describing the conscience because if the conscience isn't usually right, it would not be of much use. A compass that's unreliable is not helpful. (This criticism aside, we warmly recommend Ash's book.)

Christians are called to do much better: to cultivate conscience rather than to stifle its occasional chirps."[9]

Your conscience is not identical to the voice of God. That voice in your head is not necessarily what God would say. So how do you cultivate a conscience that aligns with God's voice? Let's briefly look at Romans 14.

Is Your Conscience Theologically Correct?

Romans 14, which we unpack in the next chapter, does not directly address how to calibrate your conscience. Rather, it instructs how to love other people in your church who have different conscience standards than you do. Romans 14 mentions three specific areas of disagreement:

1. v. 2: "One person believes he may *eat anything*, while the weak person *eats only vegetables*."
2. v. 5a: "One person *esteems one day as better than another*, while another *esteems all days alike*."
3. v. 21: "It is good not to eat meat or *drink wine* or do anything that causes your brother to stumble."

Concerning these differences, Paul refers to two groups of people in the church: the "strong" and the "weak" (Rom. 15:1; see table 2).

ISSUE IN ROMANS 14	THE "STRONG"	THE "WEAK"
1. food (vv. 2, 21)	eat all kinds of food	eat only vegetables
2. holy days (v. 5a)	make no distinction among days	value some days more than others
3. wine (v. 21; cf. v. 17)	drink wine	abstain from wine

Table 2. Three disputable matters in Romans 14[10]

---

[9] Edmund P. Clowney, *The Message of 1 Peter: The Way of the Cross*, The Bible Speaks Today (Downers Grove, IL: InterVarsity Press, 1988), 152.

[10] This table uses wording from Douglas J. Moo, *The Epistle to the Romans*, New International Commentary on the New Testament (Grand Rapids, MI: Eerdmans, 1996), 827.

For each of these issues, the position that the "strong" hold is theologically informed, and the position that the "weak" hold is theologically uninformed but not heretical. Paul himself had a strong and confident conscience on these matters (Rom. 15:1), but he never explicitly commanded the weak in conscience to change their theologically uninformed standards. He left room for a conscience that had not yet been corrected or calibrated on specific issues.

Does that mean, then, that Paul was completely neutral on whether a believer should be weak or strong in conscience? Or did he imply a preference by using the adjectives "strong" and "weak"? We think the terms "strong" and "weak" at least suggest that a strong conscience is more desirable than a weak one. Why wouldn't you want your conscience to be as scripturally informed as possible? Having said that, it's also clear from Romans 14 that the strong in faith do not necessarily please God any more than the weak in faith. Both can glorify God, and both can sin against God.

Calibrating Your Conscience

With these categories in place, we are now in a position to discuss calibrating the conscience. You probably know what it means to *calibrate* an instrument such as a scale or clock or speedometer.

After ten years as a one-car family, my wife and I (Andy) recently joined the "swagger wagon" club and bought a minivan. I soon noticed that the van's speedometer routinely reads about four miles per hour faster than the speed that our GPS indicates. I discovered that the manufacturer intentionally calibrates the speedometer to read three or four miles per hour faster than the actual speed. Even more frustrating, I can't find a way to recalibrate the speedometer other than buying larger tires. Not even the dealership will touch it.

Or let's say you weigh 110 pounds. If you step on a scale and that scale reads 115 pounds, then that scale is off by 5 pounds. Someone needs to calibrate it so it functions accurately.

That's essentially what calibrating is: aligning an instrument with a standard to ensure that it is functioning accurately. Your conscience is a part of you that functions like an instrument, and it doesn't always function accurately. So you need to calibrate your conscience to align it more closely with the standard of God's Word.

If the analogy of calibration strikes you as too mechanical, think of your conscience instead as a beautiful garden that God has prepared and given to you as a gift. But in the process of growing up in your culture and your family and your church, weeds sneak into the garden that don't belong there. And some plants that do belong end up dying. No garden can be neglected for long without such consequences.

Imagine what a jungle Paul's conscience was the day he became a Christian, with not only all of God's good rules in it but also cultural scruples and hundreds of commandments from his life as a Pharisee. But it's clear that at some point in Paul's life he opened the gate of the garden to Jesus and said, "It's yours, Lord. Tell me what stays, tell me what goes, and tell me what's missing." This is what the mature Christian must do.

As we saw in chapter 1, the most obvious of the two great principles of conscience is "obey it." Occasionally this principle collides with the other great principle of conscience: "God is the Lord of your conscience." Understanding how these two principles work together will help you understand how to calibrate your conscience.

Reasons Your Conscience May Change

Your conscience is your consciousness of what you believe is right and wrong *at any given point in time*, and it can change for a complex of reasons. You might think that something is wrong at one point in your life but think that it is right at a later point in your life. Or you might think that something is right at one point in your life but think that it is wrong at a later point in your life. Why is that? What are some reasons that your conscience may change? Here are three:

1. Your conscience might *become more hardened through the deceitfulness of sin*. Some people think that their mind is broadening, but in reality their conscience is stretching.[11] Feeding excuses to your conscience is like feeding sleeping pills to a watchdog.

2. Your conscience might *follow the standards of other people* such as your culture, family, or spiritual leaders. You simply go with the flow without thinking through issues.

3. Your conscience might *conform more to truth*, especially the truth of God's Word.

Sinning against Your Conscience vs. Calibrating Your Conscience

Because God is the Lord of your conscience, he expects you as a mature believer to gradually adjust or calibrate your conscience to match God's will as Scripture reveals it. To train and educate your conscience is not to sin against it but to put it under the lordship of Christ. To live according to your conscience brings blessing. To train your conscience to more nearly match God's truth brings even more blessing.

Here's the big question: How do you know the difference between *sinning* against your conscience and *calibrating* your conscience, since in both cases you're telling your conscience to be quiet?

1. You are *sinning* against your conscience when *you believe* your conscience is speaking correctly and yet you refuse

---

[11] See MacArthur, "How Sin Silences the Conscience," chap. 3 in *Vanishing Conscience*.

to listen to it. Emphasis on "you believe": you must obey your conscience *if you believe* it's functioning accurately. It may not be functioning accurately, but if you think it is, then you must follow it. If you think that it's wrong to drink root beer, then you are sinning if you drink root beer. As Mark Dever puts it, "Conscience cannot make a wrong thing right, but it can make a right thing wrong."[12]

2. You are *calibrating* your conscience when Christ, the Lord of your conscience, teaches you through his Scripture that your conscience has been incorrectly warning you about a particular matter, so you decide no longer to listen to your conscience in that one matter. This is calibrating or adjusting or training your conscience, not sinning against it. In the early stages of calibration, deciding not to listen to your conscience may *feel* like you're sinning against it. When you drink your first root beer after becoming completely convinced that root beer is okay, your conscience may warn you. Ignoring that warning is not searing your conscience but calibrating it under the lordship of Christ.

Does the Bible include any examples of someone calibrating their conscience? Yes. This is exactly what Peter had to do— rather quickly!—in Acts 10:

> The next day, as they were on their journey and approaching the city, Peter went up on the housetop about the sixth hour to pray. And he became hungry and wanted something to eat, but while they were preparing it, he fell into

---

[12] Mark Dever, Twitter post, August 8, 2012, https://twitter.com/MarkDever/status/2331675 17277888512. Cf. D. A. Carson, *For the Love of God: A Daily Companion for Discovering the Riches of God's Word* (Wheaton, IL: Crossway, 1998), vol. 1, Sept. 3 entry: "Paul assumes that it is wrong to go against conscience, for then conscience may be damaged ([1 Cor.] 8:12). A conscience hardened in one area, over an indifferent matter, may become hard in another area—something more crucial. Ideally, of course, the conscience should become more perfectly aligned with what God says in Scripture, so that in indifferent matters it would leave the individual free. Conscience may be instructed and shaped by truth. But until conscience has been reformed by Scripture, it is best not to contravene it."

a trance and saw the heavens opened and something like a great sheet descending, being let down by its four corners upon the earth. In it were all kinds of animals and reptiles and birds of the air. And there came a voice to him: "Rise, Peter; kill and eat." But Peter said, "By no means, Lord; for I have never eaten anything that is common or unclean." And the voice came to him again a second time, "What God has made clean, do not call common." This happened three times, and the thing was taken up at once to heaven. (Acts 10:9–16)

God gave Peter a vision of certain kinds of animals that the Old Testament forbade Jews to eat. But in the vision, the Lord Jesus said, "Kill and eat." Peter's weak conscience revolted against this command: "By no means, Lord; for I have never eaten anything that is common or unclean."[13] Clearly, Peter's faith in Christ was not weak; he was an apostle who understood and believed the gospel. Thousands had converted under his preaching, and he had even suffered for the gospel. Yet when it came to eating unclean animals and fellowshiping with Gentiles, Peter's faith was still very weak indeed, in the sense that he lacked *confidence* to do these things. But because Christ himself was commanding him, he had to calibrate his conscience so that he would have the faith (confidence) to accept food and people that he was previously not able to accept.

How Do You Calibrate Your Conscience?

So how should you calibrate your conscience? We suggest two basic principles:

1. *Calibrate your conscience by educating it with truth.* As best you can, try to discern why you hold certain convictions.

---

[13] As an interesting contrast, the prophet Ezekiel responds similarly to one of God's commands in Ezek. 4:12–15, but there God accommodates Ezekiel's conscience.

Is it based on truth, especially the truth God has revealed in Scripture? Here's how John MacArthur puts it:

> The conscience reacts to the convictions of the mind and therefore can be encouraged and sharpened in accordance with God's Word. The wise Christian wants to master biblical truth so that the conscience is completely informed and judges right because it is responding to God's Word. A regular diet of Scripture will strengthen a weak conscience or restrain an overactive one. Conversely, error, human wisdom, and wrong moral influences filling the mind will corrupt or cripple the conscience.
>
> In other words, the conscience functions like a skylight, not a light bulb. It lets light into the soul; it does not produce its own. Its effectiveness is determined by the amount of pure light we expose it to, and by how clean we keep it. Cover it or put it in total darkness and it ceases to function. That's why the apostle Paul spoke of the importance of a clear conscience (1 Tim. 3:9) and warned against anything that would defile or muddy the conscience (1 Cor. 8:7; Tit. 1:15).[14]

When we say you need to calibrate your conscience by informing your conscience with truth, we mean primarily the truth of the Bible. But it's not solely truth that appears in the Bible. Sometimes our conscience is mistaken because we've applied biblical principles the wrong way due to being misinformed about truth *outside* the Bible. For example, you might think that a particular form of birth control is acceptable but later change your conviction about it when you learn that it induces abortion. When we form convictions about what we believe is right and wrong, we must take into account truth in two spheres: (1) truth *inside* the Bible and (2) truth *outside* the Bible.

---

[14] MacArthur, *The Vanishing Conscience*, 39.

This education is not something you do in a vacuum or all alone. God has put you into a community and given you various relationships of accountability, especially your family (if you're young) and your church. Godly church leaders will help you discern the difference between issues of right and wrong and issues of preference or scruple.

2. *Calibrate your conscience with due process.* This is a wisdom issue. Sometimes it will take a lot of time to work through a particular matter. The example of Peter in Acts 10 is unusual because God directly commanded him to do something that his conscience previously prohibited him from doing. As a mature Christian, Peter was able to calibrate his conscience on the fly. But sometimes it can take us *years* to calibrate our conscience on a particular issue. And Peter's failure many years later to eat with the Gentiles in Antioch when under pressure reminds us that sometimes *re*calibration is necessary (Gal. 2:11–14).

Examples That Illustrate How You Might Calibrate Your Conscience

So how might you calibrate your conscience? Here we give some brief examples. We intentionally selected a variety of examples that fall all over the spectrum of less strict to more strict. You may be tempted to skip some of the more bizarre examples because you think they don't apply to you, but we think it would be best if you didn't. At the very least, they'll serve as thought experiments that will help you think through how to deal with other issues you are wrestling with, and they'll remind you of how important it is to be forbearing with those who have rules that strike you as strange (more on that in the next chapter).

The reason we are sharing these examples is not to persuade you to adopt our particular convictions. We're not devoting sufficient space to persuasively argue for our positions. Nor will we go into great detail about how *due process* involves reading and meditating on Scripture, processing wisdom from your church's elders and other Christians, and proceeding cautiously and prayerfully.

Rather, we are sharing these examples merely to illustrate what it might look like to calibrate your conscience. You may disagree with our convictions on various issues, and that's fine. We think we're right (otherwise we wouldn't hold these convictions!), but we could be wrong. And we always want to remain open to calibrating our conscience so that it better aligns with God's will. The purpose of this chapter is to teach you how to calibrate *your* individual conscience. Later chapters will address how to relate to other people when your consciences disagree.

As you'll see, we include some personal examples of when we've had to calibrate or train or reeducate our consciences. Bear in mind that some of our examples reflect our cultural locations. For example, Andy has lived in the United States his entire life, and J. D. has lived in Asian cultures nearly his entire life. Again, in a later chapter we will see how cultural context plays a major role in defining debates related to conscience; here we get a taste of that dynamic.

There are two basic ways to calibrate an instrument using two basic methods: by adding to it or subtracting from it. For example, if your scale reads 115 pounds when it should say 120 pounds, then you need to calibrate that scale by *adding* 5 pounds. But if your scale reads 115 pounds when it should say 110 pounds, then you need to calibrate that scale by *subtracting* 5 pounds. We'll use these two categories for basic ways that you can calibrate your conscience: adding to your conscience and subtracting from your conscience. (Of course, in most situations, conscience calibration involves both addition and subtraction; adding a restriction to your conscience often means subtracting the corresponding freedom and vice versa.)

Adding to Your Conscience

Sometimes we need to calibrate our conscience by adding commands to it. Something's missing that ought to be there. Our conscience may be malfunctioning because we've deeply absorbed the sinful worldview of this age. Many people live together with their boyfriend or girlfriend with a clear conscience or look at pornography with a clear conscience. Many men and women abort their babies with a clear conscience. Many people gossip with a clear conscience. Many people tell all sorts of lies with a clear conscience. Many people get drunk with a clear conscience. What needs to change? They need to calibrate their conscience by educating it with truth: (1) Sexual immorality is a sin against God and others. (2) Abortion is murder. (3) Gossip is sin. (4) Lying is sin. (5) Getting drunk is a sin.

Just because you can sin with a clear conscience doesn't mean that what you're doing is okay. If a police officer pulls you over for going eighty miles per hour in a forty-mile-per-hour zone, do you think he'll let you go if you appeal, "But officer, my speedometer indicated that I was going only forty miles per hour"? "That's *your* problem," he'd say. "Calibrate your speedometer." When it comes to sin, you're responsible to calibrate your conscience.

When else might you calibrate your conscience by *adding* to it?

1. *Should you view sexually charged nudity in videos?* Your conscience may allow you to view sexually charged nudity in videos, but that alone does not make it right. Although some defend this practice in certain situations,[15] we have yet to hear a convincing defense. We think that, at best, it is extremely

---

[15] E.g., John M. Frame, *The Doctrine of the Christian Life*, A Theology of Lordship (Phillipsburg, NJ: P&R, 2008), 895–96.

unwise to watch explicit nudity and that we should completely avoid viewing it.[16]

2. *How far is too far in a dating relationship? Should unmarried people passionately kiss each other or have nonintercourse sex?* Many unmarried people practice these activities, and some do it with a clear conscience. Perhaps you're in a dating relationship with someone right now, and your passions are raging to have a physical relationship with your girlfriend or boyfriend. You may even be engaged to be married. You know that the Bible limits sex exclusively to marriage, but you are flirting with the idea of getting as close as possible to that line while technically remaining a virgin. But we think that a rightly calibrated conscience will guide you to reserve all forms of sexual activity—including passionate kissing—for marriage.[17]

3. *Is it okay to use certain forms of reproductive technologies and other forms of genetic engineering such as gene therapy and stem cell technology?* To form convictions about bioethics, you have to understand truth in two spheres: *in* the Bible and *outside* the Bible. I (Andy) recently calibrated my conscience in this area by adding truth from *outside* the Bible when some members of my church expanded my knowledge of such procedures. Paul and Susan Lim understand medicine. Paul is a plastic surgeon, and Susan is a pediatrician. When the Lims spoke in my school's chapel in 2014 about their embryo adoption, they helped me to educate my conscience with truth that I previously didn't know.[18] Another member of my church, Matt Anderson,

---

[16] We recommend John Piper's twelve diagnostic questions about this issue: "12 Questions to Ask Before You Watch 'Game of Thrones,'" *Desiring God Blog*, June 20, 2014, http://www.desiringgod.org/blog/posts/12-questions-to-ask-before-you-watch-game-of-thrones.

[17] See Gerald Hiestand, "A Biblical-Theological Approach to Premarital Sexual Ethics: or, What Saint Paul Would Say about 'Making Out,'" *Bulletin of Ecclesial Theology* 1 (2014): 13–32, which expounds on the first two chapters in Gerald Hiestand and Jay Thomas, *Sex, Dating, and Relationships: A Fresh Approach* (Wheaton, IL: Crossway, 2012).

[18] "Paul and Susan Lim—Embryo Adoption," Bethlehem College and Seminary, February 3, 2014, http://vimeo.com/85750326. Cf. their abbreviated testimony: "Fearfully and Wonderfully Made: The Miracle of Madeleine," Bethlehem Baptist Church, January 24, 2015, https://vimeo.com/117688402.

MD, has been an ob-gyn for over thirty years, and *WORLD Magazine* has published several of his articles. Both Dr. Anderson and the Lims have helped me educate my conscience that people cannot be pro-life and practice *in vitro* fertilization.

4. *Should I spend a lot of time on sports (or other hobbies)?* I (Andy) was a sports fanatic as a child. I would get up before anyone else in my home, grab the newspaper at the end of the driveway, and read the sports section cover to cover. I played baseball, basketball, football, and hockey. I had large collections of sports cards. I subscribed to sports magazines, hung posters of sports players on my bedroom wall, and watched games on TV as often as I could.

Sports and most other hobbies are not sinful in and of themselves. The real issue is not sports but the proper use of time for a Christian. In high school, when I grew more serious about following Jesus as my master, I realized my conscience was missing the category of *wasting time on unnecessary pursuits*. Sports are not inherently sinful, but what if all those not-necessarily-sinful activities add up to a life that lacks time for more important activities? I felt convicted that sports were eating up too much of my time. So I pulled back.

I have absolutely no regrets about that calibration. I still follow some sports casually and occasionally watch a game. But my conscience won't let me give myself wholeheartedly to sports like that again, or to any other time-sucking hobby, because I'm convinced that it's not the best way for me to spend the short life that God has given me.

At the same time, I have good friends who passionately follow sports and see them as an opportunity for spending time with family, friends, and neighbors. For some, sports are their main outlet for actively engaging with their community. In that case, following sports ceases to be a waste of time and instead strategically uses time for God's glory. This scenario illustrates that mature Christians may form different convictions about specific issues.

These examples involve adding commands to your conscience that should have been there, but sometimes you need to calibrate your conscience not by addition but by subtraction.

Subtracting from Your Conscience

I (Andy) drive an old Buick that perpetually has the "Service engine" light on. It has been like that for about the last year. When that warning light used to come on, it usually meant something significant, and once I took care of the problem, the warning light would go off. But about a year ago this light just wouldn't turn off. My mechanic told me not to worry because the light is oversensitive about something unimportant (though he did say to let him know if the light ever started *blinking*). Sometimes your conscience's warning light comes on because it is oversensitive about something that is not wrong. But rather than live in a perpetual state of going against your conscience, you must train your conscience. When might you calibrate your conscience by *subtracting unnecessary rules* from it?

1. *Should you get a tattoo?* Tattoos were generally frowned upon among previous generations, but they are now becoming increasingly common. According to some studies, about 40 percent of adults ages 18–40 in the United States have a tattoo. And many Christians today get tattoos with a clear conscience. But should they?

Answering that question isn't as simple as quoting the Bible's only explicit reference to tattooing: "You shall not make any cuts on your body for the dead or tattoo yourselves: I am the LORD" (Lev. 19:28). Christians are no longer under the Mosaic law-covenant,[19] and tattoos in Moses's ancient Near Eastern

---

[19] See Thomas R. Schreiner, *40 Questions about Christians and Biblical Law*, 40 Questions (Grand Rapids, MI: Kregel, 2010), probably the single best introduction to this complex issue.

context communicated something much different than they do in many places today. So we don't think it's inherently sinful to have a tattoo today. We've taken this issue out of the category of moral right and wrong in our own hearts and placed it into a category of freedom.

So did we immediately go out and get a YHWH tattoo on our forearm? We didn't. Why not? Because life isn't about us. It's about Christ and the gospel. As we'll learn in more detail in chapter 6, we need to think about other things besides just our freedom to do something hip and cool. And for us, this is the most important: *A tattoo could make us less missional.* There are places all over the world where having a tattoo could limit our ministry for the sake of the gospel. In the majority world, most people still associate tattoos with sorcery and the occult, believing they give a person some strength over evil spirits and curses. We don't know what kind of mission work God may have for us later in our lives. Is it wise to cut off opportunities to spread the gospel?[20] That reasoning is decisive for us not to get tattoos.[21] But dear Christian friends of ours have tattoos, and we are not judgmental toward them. In fact, we know of a Christian in California who uses his Scripture tattoos as opportunities for witness. He's a walking gospel billboard.

One more observation: Our position on tattoos illustrates that someone can have a strong, free conscience on a particular issue and yet choose to act in a way that is externally indistinguishable from someone with a weaker, stricter conscience. Think of two groups of believers. One group is theologically

---

[20] John Piper made a similar argument in his "Ask Pastor John" podcasts on December 19–20, 2013: "Tattoos in Biblical Perspective," Episode 240, https://soundcloud.com/askpastorjohn/tattoos-in-biblical; "Six Reasons to Skip Tattoos," Episode 241, https://soundcloud.com/askpastorjohn/six-reasons-to-skip-tattoos.

[21] One might consider practical matters as well: Your body will change over the next several decades, and so will that tattoo. Do you really want those markings on your skin *permanently*? And your tastes may change: what you think is artsy and attractive now may strike you as dull or ugly or immature later. But these considerations are way down the list in importance for us.

correct in believing that it is morally acceptable to have a tattoo today; the other group is theologically incorrect in believing that it is inherently sinful to have a tattoo. Yet both groups choose not to get tattoos. Functionally, they act the same on this matter, but what undergirds their decisions is significantly different. We are arguing that though we are free to get tattoos, we think that, for us, it is wisest to refrain from getting them for a complex of reasons, the most decisive reason being missional. We are trying to be like Paul in 1 Corinthians 9:19–23. (More on this principle in chapter 6.)

2. *Is it sinful to use certain instruments in congregational worship?* I (J. D.) live and work in a tribal area of Cambodia. The most important musical instrument in many tribes of Southeast Asia is the brass gong. A set of gongs consists of five larger rhythm gongs of various sizes (the largest being nearly three feet across!) and eight smaller melody gongs played much like bells in a bell choir in the West. The sound is deep, lush, and captivating. But when we suggested to the new believers that they use the gongs to worship the true God, they unanimously rejected the idea. Gongs were so strongly associated in their minds with demon worship that their conscience would not let them use gongs to worship God.

Because we understood the workings of conscience, we didn't push the matter, but we did remind them when opportunities arose that everything good belongs to God, including the gongs—even music itself belongs to God (Zeph. 3:17). Satan stole these good things for his evil purposes. "Someday," we said, "when your consciences grow strong, you might decide to use these beautiful instruments to praise the true and living God."

A few years later the leaders approached us and said it was time. They had educated their consciences with God's truth that "the earth is the Lord's, and the fullness thereof" (1 Cor.

10:26; cf. Ps. 24:1). So they subtracted from their conscience the conviction that it is inherently sinful to worship God with gongs. They set a day, and dozens of tribal believers gathered from many villages to play gongs and write new songs to praise the true and living God. Fifteen years later in some villages, only the Christians use gongs anymore; the unbelievers have sold theirs to buy motorcycles and TVs!

By the way, this example shows us that a person can acquire a weak conscience on a particular issue simply through former associations. The conscience of some of the new believers in Corinth restrained them from eating any meat at all, not because of their strict upbringing (as in the case of those with a weak conscience in Romans 14), but because eating meat was so closely associated with pagan ritual sacrifice that they couldn't eat meat without thinking of those gods (1 Corinthians 8).[22]

3. *Is it sinful to listen to particular styles of music?* I (Andy) grew up in church contexts where my godly Christian leaders taught that particular styles of music—especially contemporary music—inherently communicate sinful sensuality and rebellion in all times and all cultures. It took me a few years to work through this one because it was so deeply ingrained in my conscience. But since I've educated my conscience with truth about the nature of music and how its cultural associations can change over time, this is no longer a conscience issue for me.

I have many good friends who have more strict convictions on this issue, and I deeply respect them and their convictions. We agree with truth *in the Bible* that God's people should be holy and not worldly. But we disagree on how we understand truth *outside the Bible* regarding the nature of music, its associations, and its inherent connotations.

---

[22] Yet another way to acquire a weak conscience is to be born with an overconscientious, timid personality that tends to feel guilt or doubt no matter what you do.

4. *Is it sinful to celebrate Halloween?* When I (Andy) was a young child, my family celebrated Halloween each year. We would dress up in costumes and go door-to-door in our neighborhood to get candy from neighbors, and we would hand out candy from our front door to neighbors who came by.

But we later stopped doing that. Instead, we would turn out all the lights and go eat pizza and play games at Chuck E. Cheese. Part of the reasoning, I think, is that some Christian friends with good intentions suggested that Halloween was associated with the occult and that anything associated with Halloween was therefore Satanic. So we shouldn't participate in it at all. As a kid I thought, "Fair enough. And I like Chuck E. Cheese." It was a win-win for me. But this practice of not celebrating Halloween eventually became a conscience issue for me, a matter of right and wrong.

Choosing not to celebrate Halloween because of its associations is a viable position, but my wife, Jenni, and I have now decided that it's not the most strategic. In our experience most of our neighbors celebrate Halloween with fall and harvest themes and don't think of it as a Satanic holiday. So we do celebrate Halloween each year in a minimalist way: we dress up our kids, perhaps as Little Bo Peep or their favorite animal; we go door-to-door in our neighborhood to get candy; and we give away candy at our front door. It's an enjoyable family tradition.

But more important, we think it's a strategic cultural tradition. What other day of the year are all our neighbors *expecting* us to knock on their doors? It's a time to make and renew personal connections with neighbors for the sake of the gospel. In a culture where garage doors often function like castle gates, we jump at the opportunity to interact face-to-face with our neighbors in a friendly, nonconfrontational way.

5. *Is it sinful to bite your fingernails?* We're using this particular issue to illustrate a profound concept: the difference

between Bible rules and family or cultural rules, such as making your bed in the morning or practicing pristine hygiene.

We have heard some American adults say that they grew up thinking that biting your fingernails was wrong. Their parents ingrained in them over and over, "Don't bite your fingernails." So even as adults they would look at other people biting their fingernails and think, "I can't believe they are doing that. That is so wrong." What happened? The parents had a reasonable family rule ("Don't bite your fingernails"), but they didn't distinguish family rules from Bible rules.

There is a big difference between a family rule like "Don't bite your fingernails" and a biblical command like "Speak truthfully." The Bible doesn't command you not to bite your fingernails; the Bible *does* command you to speak truthfully and not lie.

But when parents tell their children not to bite their fingernails, children sometimes misconstrue the biblical principle as "I must not bite my fingernails because *God says* not to bite my fingernails." Instead, the parents should help children understand the rule as "I must not bite my fingernails because my parents are asking me not to bite my nails, and I must obey my parents when what they command does not contradict Scripture."

If we don't distinguish family rules from Bible commands, our children will tend to lump them all into the same category. Not only will they clutter their conscience with unnecessary taboos, they will have a difficult time processing why other Christian families and Christians in other cultures follow different rules. It may tempt them to reject all rules later in life instead of simply adjusting their consciences as they get older.[23]

---

[23] And when rules like that become embedded in your conscience, you may misinterpret the Bible to make it support your view. Here's an embarrassing example. When I (Andy) was in eighth grade, the youth pastor of our small church asked me to give a devotional to the youth group on a Wednesday evening. I don't remember what my train of thought was, but it must

Of course, it's almost impossible to keep our children from turning family rules into matters of conscience. I (J. D.) would tell my kids over and over that these rules were not moral issues but simply family conventions or matters of hygiene, but the rules still wormed their way into their already overpacked consciences. However, the repeated reminders eventually bore fruit. When our children got older and began the task of calibrating their own consciences, the distinctions my wife and I tried to make early on helped them sift through their list of rules.

6. *Is it sinful for guys to wear shorts or jeans?* Don't roll your eyes. This question may make you "face palm" in amazement at how strange someone else's conscience might be. That's typically how someone with a strong conscience reacts when they hear about the scruples of the weak. But to the weak of conscience, these are life-and-death matters. Conscience is always a life-and-death matter since sinning against it is always a sin, and getting used to sinning against conscience in one area will make it easier to sin against conscience in other areas. The strong must not look down on the weak but bear with them (Rom. 15:1) and, if opportunity arises, gently help them calibrate their conscience. But more on that in chapter 5.

Back to this issue of shorts and jeans. When I (Andy) was a child, my family was for a time part of a very culturally conservative church that held unusually strict dress standards. Among other things, they thought it was best if guys didn't wear shorts or jeans. In their minds, shorts were immodest and jeans were historically associated with rebellion and sexual immorality. So whether guys were exercising or mowing the lawn or playing

---

have been something like this: "What is something that I can say to my peers? I've been to their homes, and some of them live like slobs. Hmmm. I know what to speak on!" So the first devotional I ever gave was on why you should keep your room clean. I'm not kidding. But it gets worse. The text I chose to support my argument was 1 Corinthians 14:40: "All things should be done decently and in order." In case you didn't know, that passage of Scripture isn't talking about why you should keep your room clean. And my youth pastor kindly and wisely let me know that in front of my peers after I finished.

basketball, they wore either nylon wind pants or khakis. That struck me as really odd at first, but I wanted to be a good Christian, so I followed suit. Eventually, this rule made its way into my conscience.

After I moved away from that subculture to a slightly less conservative subculture, it took me a little while to calibrate my conscience under the lordship of Christ and accept that it was not wrong for me to wear shorts or jeans. To form accurate convictions, we need to rightly educate our conscience with truth both inside and outside the Bible. In this case I removed this taboo from my conscience by simply educating my conscience with truth from outside the Bible. In American culture, shorts or jeans on guys simply don't convey immodesty, rebellion, or sexual immorality in and of themselves.

Other Issues about Which You Might Need
to Calibrate Your Conscience
We could easily multiply examples:

1. watching mixed martial arts for entertainment
2. how to treat Sundays
3. listening to "secular" music
4. dressing modestly
5. capitalism vs. socialism
6. fair-trade coffee
7. global warming
8. watching particular movies or TV shows
9. playing video games
10. reading J. K. Rowling's *Harry Potter* series
11. ladies wearing makeup
12. following the schedule in *Growing Kids God's Way*
13. homeopathic medicine vs. antibiotics
14. public school vs. private school vs. private Christian school vs. homeschool

15. eating fast food that is unhealthy[24]
16. a church with multiple services and multiple sites
17. Christian hip-hop
18. body piercings
19. smoking cigars
20. drinking alcohol in moderation
21. going into debt
22. dating vs. courtship
23. when married couples should start trying to have children
24. how many children married couples should have
25. practicing daily family devotions
26. being overweight
27. perpetuating the Santa Claus myth

But we don't want to get too controversial! You won't find two Christians on the face of the earth who agree entirely about every matter of conscience. Many will even debate whether some of these matters should be on a list of issues that might require calibration! We have shared some of our convictions, but in this book we haven't taken a view on most of the above issues, let alone defended those convictions. Instead, our goal here is merely to illustrate that you must take the time and effort—the due process—to calibrate your conscience by educating your conscience with truth.[25]

Why You Should Not Be Dogmatic about All Your Convictions

D. Martyn Lloyd-Jones was one of the greatest preachers of the twentieth century, and we esteem him highly. But in March 1924, when he was twenty-four years old, he shared some

---

[24] Though what if it's Chick-fil-A—*Christian* fast food?

[25] Many of John Piper's "Ask Pastor John" podcasts address issues like these, invariably with wisdom that combines truth inside the Bible and truth outside the Bible. See http://www .desiringgod.org/interviews/by-series/ask-pastor-john.

convictions (i.e., firmly held opinions) in a way that we suspect he later regretted. His statement is instructive for the rest of us:

> I cannot possibly understand a man who wears silk stockings or even gaudily coloured socks; rings, wrist-watches, spats, shoes instead of boots, or who carries a cane in his hand. . . . The modern method of installing a bath in each house is not only a tragedy but it has been a real curse to humanity. . . . If I had to spend a life-time with a companion who had one bath a day or with one who had one bath a year, I should unhesitatingly choose the latter, because a man's soul is more important than his skin. . . . When I enter a house and find that they have a wireless apparatus [i.e., a radio] I know at once that there is something wrong. . . . Your five-valve sets may do wonders, they may enable you to hear the voice of America, but believe me, they will never transmit the only Voice that is worth listening to.[26]

This may make you laugh today, but you have probably made similar judgmental statements that later embarrassed you. This story illustrates why you should avoid being dogmatic about all your convictions. Sometimes your convictions are based on a misinformed conscience that you need to calibrate.

We must do this careful process of calibration in the context of biblical and theological training in the church. A theologically uninformed believer, explains D. A. Carson, runs the risk of jettisoning from his conscience laws that Scripture clearly teaches:

> Although Paul was an extraordinarily flexible apostle and evangelist, he had sorted through elemental Christianity in a profound and nuanced way so that he knew when he could be flexible and when he should not bend. In other

[26] Quoted in Iain H. Murray, *D. Martyn Lloyd-Jones: The First Forty Years, 1899–1939* (Edinburgh: Banner of Truth, 1982), 65–66.

words, his grasp of theology enabled him to know who he was, what was expected of him, what he was free to do, and what he should not consider doing under any circumstances.

In short, we must also know what freedoms and constraints are ours in Jesus Christ. The only way to achieve this maturity is to think through Scripture again and again to try to grasp the system of its thought—how the parts cohere and combine to make sense.[27]

We have been addressing a very specific issue: how you as an *individual* should calibrate your conscience. But how should you relate to other people when your consciences disagree?

---

[27] D. A. Carson, *The Cross and Christian Ministry: An Exposition of Passages from 1 Corinthians* (Grand Rapids, MI: Baker, 1993), 120–21.

5

HOW SHOULD YOU RELATE TO FELLOW CHRISTIANS WHEN YOUR CONSCIENCES DISAGREE?

This is where the book turns from focusing on just you and your individual conscience to how your conscience relates to others. The complexity of conscience-related problems rises exponentially when you move from an individual to a group of people—and so do the stakes. This complexity explains why this is the book's most dense chapter. But the high stakes make it essential for you to patiently slog through these principles of how to get along with people who have differing consciences.

How should you relate to other people with differing consciences, especially family members and church members? What do you do when your conscience allows you to do certain practices but another person's conscience does not? What do you do when your conscience does *not* allow you to do certain practices but another person's conscience does?

Theological Triage

You've probably experienced triage if you've ever visited an emergency room. Let's say that on a Friday night you break your leg. When you arrive at the emergency room, about twenty other people are already sitting around. You check in, have a seat, and wait . . . and wait. Thirty minutes pass. You must be getting close. Then all of a sudden, another person arrives on a stretcher—an hour after you did—and he gets immediate medical attention because he was just in a horrific car accident. Why does he get to cut in line? You were there first! This is an example of *medical* triage: assigning degrees of urgency to wounds or illnesses to decide in what order to treat a large number of patients. Triage is the action of sorting according to priority and urgency.

We understand that sometimes we have to prioritize. Some things are more pressing and more important than other things. My wife, Jenni, and I (Andy) have three little girls, and sometimes all of them are crying at the same time. We have to prioritize their needs according to urgency. We might call that *parental* triage.

Did you know that this is also the case with truths that the Bible teaches? We could call it *theological* triage.[1] Some Bible teachings are more important than other Bible teachings. As Paul writes in 1 Corinthians 15:3, "I delivered to you as of *first importance* what I also received." The words "first importance" imply that although everything in the Bible is important, not everything is *equally* important. Some doctrines are *more* important. To simplify things, we could think of three levels of theological triage:

---

[1] See, e.g., R. Albert Mohler Jr., "Confessional Evangelicalism," in *Four Views on the Spectrum of Evangelicalism*, ed. Andrew David Naselli and Collin Hansen, Counterpoints: Bible and Theology (Grand Rapids, MI: Zondervan, 2011), 77–80. Some people refer to these three levels as (1) dogma, (2) doctrine, and (3) differences; or (1) absolutes, (2) convictions, and (3) opinions and questions; or (1) essential, (2) important, and (3) nonessential.

First-level issues are most central and essential to Christianity. You can't *deny* these teachings and still be a Christian in any meaningful sense. For example, there is one God in three persons; Jesus is fully God and fully human; Jesus sacrificially died for sinners; Jesus rose bodily from the dead; we are justified by grace alone through faith alone in Christ alone; Jesus is coming back.

Second-level issues create reasonable boundaries between Christians, such as different denominations and local churches. These issues will have a bearing on what sort of church you are part of. For example, what's your view on baptism or church government or God's sovereignty in salvation or the role of men and women in the church and home? You don't have to hold one particular view to be a Christian, but it's challenging for a church to have a healthy unity when its leaders and members disagree on these matters.

Third-level issues are disputable matters (also called matters of indifference or matters of *conscience*). They might involve how you interpret particular passages of the Bible. For example, who are "the sons of God" in Genesis 6? There is more than one viable view. Third-level issues also include many practical questions. For example, how should Christians view the "Sabbath"? Is it okay on Sundays to go to a public restaurant? Or shop at a grocery store? Or watch a football game? Or *play* a football game? Or mow your lawn? Or work for pay? Disputable matters aren't unimportant, but members of the same church should be able to disagree on these issues and still have close fellowship with each other. Disagreement on third-level issues shouldn't cause disunity in the church family.

It's easy for third-level matters to become deeply ingrained in someone's conscience. And wherever two or more people interact in some sort of relationship—whether they are siblings, fellow students, coworkers, neighbors, or church members—

they will dispute some issues. No two (finite and fallen) humans will ever agree on absolutely everything—not even a godly husband and godly wife who are happily married. We all have different perspectives, backgrounds, personalities, preferences, thought processes, and levels of understanding truth about God and his Word and his world.

So can you guess what happens when a group of self-professed Christians joins together as a church—even a doctrinally robust, gospel-centered church? They will disagree about many matters. We should *expect* disagreements with fellow Christians about third-level matters, and we should learn to live with those differences. Christians don't always need to eliminate differences, but they should always seek to glorify God by loving each other in their differences. Understanding what the conscience is and how it works helps us do that.

Conscience Controversies in the Early Church

One text in particular addresses this very question: Romans 14:1–15:7. In the greatest letter ever written in the history of the world, Paul spends about 10 percent of his time addressing the subject of conscience controversies within the church. We do well to give it the same kind of attention. This passage is brilliant. It's profound. It displays God's great knowledge and insight. Understanding and applying the principles in this passage of Scripture should make you marvel at God's wisdom.

The disputable matters that concern us today almost never *exactly* parallel what Paul addresses in this passage, but the principles in this passage directly apply to our time.[2] Before we can apply these principles to our specific contexts, though, we

---

[2] Douglas J. Moo notes: "But the value of this section is not limited to Paul's advice on these specific issues. For Paul here sets forth principles that are applicable to a range of issues that we may loosely classify as *adiaphora*: matters neither required of Christians nor prohibited to them." *The Epistle to the Romans*, New International Commentary on the New Testament (Grand Rapids, MI: Eerdmans, 1996), 881.

need to understand the nature of the disagreements that Paul addressed in his day. As we explore the situation in Romans, we will also consider related passages, such as 1 Corinthians 8–10, Galatians 2, and Colossians 2.

A typical church in Paul's day consisted of both Jewish and Gentile Christians. Coming from a religious culture that put a high premium on eating food that only the law of Moses allowed, most Jewish Christians carried that strictness into their new faith. Most Gentiles, on the other hand, had no such background. So a typical church had two groups, as table 3 shows:

STRONG CONSCIENCE	WEAK CONSCIENCE
Conscience has confidence to eat meat	Conscience lacks confidence to eat meat
"Everything belongs to God, so we can eat anything we want."	"We want to keep some of our previous food restrictions."
Mostly Gentile Christians	Mostly Jewish Christians

Table 3. The strong and the weak

The strong-weak distinction that Paul makes does not necessarily line up with a strong or weak conscience for every third-level issue, but it does for many of them, including the issues in Romans 14. The tables in this section highlight just one of the issues: eating meat (14:2). But the Jewish Christians and Gentile Christians in Rome also disagreed about holy days (14:5) and drinking wine (14:21; cf. 14:17).[3]

Regarding meat and holy days, the "weak in faith" were most likely a group of mainly Jewish Christians. This is

the one passage in Romans in which it appears that Paul has a specific problem in mind (14:1–15:13). This section rebukes two groups for their intolerance toward each other: the

---

[3] See table 2 in chapter 4.

"weak in faith" (probably mainly Jewish Christians) and the "strong in faith" (probably mainly Gentile Christians). The rebuke focuses on the Gentile Christians, who are becoming arrogant toward the shrinking minority of Jewish Christians. . . . [So] one of Paul's purposes in writing this letter was to heal this division in the Christian community in Rome.[4]

Doug Moo explains,

> The weak were influenced by a Jewish tradition of asceticism based on the torah. . . . Jewish Christians in Rome, convinced that the torah was still authoritative for Christians, claimed that a sincere Christian should avoid meat and wine and should observe the Sabbath and Jewish holy days. Only by following such practices could a Christian avoid ritual contamination and please God.[5]

Had the two sides been content to live with these differences, Paul might never have felt the need to write Romans 14. But human nature being what it is, some from both sides went too far and began to impose their freedoms or scruples on others (see table 4):

STRONG CONSCIENCE	WEAK CONSCIENCE
Conscience has confidence to eat meat	Conscience lacks confidence to eat meat
"I have freedom to eat meat, and those who don't eat meat are being unreasonable and are theologically in error."	"It's sinful to eat meat, and Christians who do so are being unfaithful to God."
Arrogance	Judgmentalism

Table 4. Potential conflict between the strong and the weak

---

[4] D. A. Carson and Douglas J. Moo, *Introducing the New Testament: A Short Guide to Its History and Message*, ed. Andrew David Naselli (Grand Rapids, MI: Zondervan, 2010), 83–84.
[5] Douglas J. Moo, *Encountering the Book of Romans: A Theological Survey*, 2nd ed., Encountering Biblical Studies (Grand Rapids, MI: Baker, 2014), 180.

Ethnic harmony in Christ was among Paul's highest concerns. It would have been disastrous if the churches had divided over issues related to ethnicity. And you can be sure that Satan, who is always looking for a split in the log, would bring his axe right down on this crack.

Seeds of Heresy to the Right and to the Left

But disunity wasn't the only danger. Seeds of outright heresy began to germinate on both sides of the controversy. In Corinth some of the believers with a strong conscience grew overconfident and had the gall to accept invitations to the banqueting halls connected to the pagan temples (see 1 Corinthians 8–10). This was quite tempting because meat was a luxury; a pagan feast might provide their protein fix for the entire month. We're pretty sure these Christians were attending only for the food and friendship and didn't even pay attention to the little opening ceremony that some pagan priest presided over. He said some meaningless chant and presented some of the meat to some empty idol. It didn't have any more meaning than a prayer before a football game in Texas. But Paul had to tell those careless believers in 1 Corinthians 10 that their participation at this event wasn't meaningless. Behind the empty idols were demons vying for their loyalty. Just by being there, these Christians were actually participating in what Paul called demon communion. We have the Lord's Supper, and they have Satan's supper (1 Cor. 10:19–21). Paul condemned this overconfidence in the strongest way (1 Cor. 10:12).

When we see the "strong" in Corinth swerve like this into lawlessness, we're tempted to think that it's best just to play it safe and err on the strict side. But the strict fell into heresies as well. In Galatia, some of the strict believers went so far as to insist that if people didn't obey the Mosaic food and circumcision laws, they couldn't be Christians at all (see Acts 15:1;

Galatians 1–2). The Bible calls these false teachers Judaizers or "the circumcision party" (Gal. 2:12). It was a heresy that brought down Paul's severest condemnation: "Let [them] be accursed" (Gal. 1:9).

So eventually the early churches began to see not only two overreactions concerning meat and other issues (the two *inner* columns in table 5) but two potential heresies as well (the two *outer* columns in table 5). None of these four positions led to peace and edification:

STRONG CONSCIENCE	STRONG CONSCIENCE	WEAK CONSCIENCE	WEAK CONSCIENCE
Strong conscience but carelessly crossing the line into lawlessness and immorality	Strong conscience but looking down on (despising) those with a weak conscience	Weak conscience but judging those with a strong conscience	Weak conscience but crossing the line into legalism
"I have freedom not only to eat meat but to go to parties at idol temples." (cf. 1 Cor. 10:20–22)	"I have freedom to eat meat, and those who don't are being unreasonable and are theologically in error."	"It's sinful to eat meat, and Christians who do so are being unfaithful to God."	"You must follow the Old Testament dietary restrictions if you want to be a Christian."
Heresy	Arrogance	Judgmentalism	Heresy
Distorts the gospel by lawless subtraction	Diminishes the gospel	Diminishes the gospel	Distorts the gospel by legalistic addition

Table 5. Seeds of heresy among the strong and the weak (two outer columns)

Paul saw the gap growing wider and wider. What would he do to keep these disagreements from destroying the unity of the churches? Paul was an apostle, so he could have easily solved this specific controversy in the church at Rome with a blanket command like this: "If you have a weak conscience, you must mature and start eating meat. Enjoy what God gives you to enjoy." After all, that was Paul's own position (Rom. 14:14). But this solution would have ignored the danger of compelling Christians to sin against their conscience, even a misinformed conscience. Mature Christians should help other Christians train their consciences, but no one should force others to change their conscience.

Or Paul could have given the opposite command: "If you have a strong conscience, you must stop eating meat entirely since exercising your freedom might affect those with a weak conscience." Many conservative churches today land here. But this solution denies believers their freedom to enjoy God's good bounty and might even cross the line into false teaching:

> Now the Spirit expressly says that in later times some will depart from the faith by devoting themselves to deceitful spirits and teachings of demons, through the insincerity of liars whose consciences are seared, who forbid marriage and require abstinence from foods that God created to be received with thanksgiving by those who believe and know the truth. For everything created by God is good, and nothing is to be rejected if it is received with thanksgiving, for it is made holy by the word of God and prayer. (1 Tim. 4:1–4)

It doesn't do any good to be stricter than God![6]

Rather than lay down a law, Paul appealed to love. His concern was unity, and ours should be too. Doug Moo puts it well:

> One of the most important points in Romans 14 is something that Paul does not say: that the weak in faith must

---

[6] See John Murray, "The Weak and the Strong," *Westminster Theological Journal* 12, no. 2 (1950): 153; Craig Blomberg, *1 Corinthians*, NIV Application Commentary (Grand Rapids, MI: Zondervan, 1994), 169; Gordon D. Fee, *The First Epistle to the Corinthians*, 2nd ed., New International Commentary on the New Testament (Grand Rapids, MI: Eerdmans, 2014), 432, 530, 541.

change their view. He makes clear that he does not agree with them, and by labeling them weak he implies also that they have room to grow on these matters. But he does not tell them to change their mind; he does not berate them for being "immature"; he does not tell them to "get with the program."

Yet this is usually our first reaction to someone who differs with us. We want to change their minds, to convince them we are right. Paul would undoubtedly support the church's efforts to educate its members as fully as possible about the gospel and its implications. But he is wise enough to know that there is a time and a place for such efforts. . . . All of us have our traditions, and they are not easy to give up. As long as they are not contrary to the gospel and hindering the work of the church, we should learn to tolerate these differences.[7]

What was Paul's solution? How would he bind these two potential factions together? His solution was love, not law. Table 6 inserts Paul's threefold solution in the place of the growing split between those with a strong conscience and those with a weak conscience. Only the three center columns please God and result in unity. On any given disagreement over disputable matters, God calls us to land on one of these three positions. God forbids the attitudes of those described in the two far left columns who look down on the strict and those described in the two far right columns who judge those with freedoms. (Don't let the size of the chart discourage you. Taking time to work your way through it will help you to understand the important issues of Romans 14 and 1 Corinthians 8–10 and to discern where your own conscience falls on this spectrum.)

---

[7] Douglas J. Moo, *Romans*, NIV Application Commentary (Grand Rapids, MI: Zondervan, 2000), 467.

PAUL'S SOLUTION OF LOVE

STRONG CONSCIENCE	STRONG CONSCIENCE	STRONG CONSCIENCE (1)	STRONG CONSCIENCE (2)	WEAK CONSCIENCE (3)	WEAK CONSCIENCE	WEAK CONSCIENCE
but carelessly crossing the line into lawlessness and immorality	but looking down on (despising) those with a weak conscience	fully persuaded, yet welcoming rather than looking down on those with a weak conscience	but free to be flexible in disputable matters in order to (1) edify fellow believers and (2) advance the gospel	fully persuaded, yet welcoming rather than judging those with a strong conscience	but judging those with a strong conscience	but crossing the line into legalism
EATS MEAT	EATS MEAT	EATS MEAT	FLEXIBLE	DOESN'T EAT MEAT	DOESN'T EAT MEAT	DOESN'T EAT MEAT
"I have freedom not only to eat meat but to go to parties at idol temples." (cf. 1 Cor. 10:20–22)	"I have freedom to eat meat, and those who don't are being unreasonable and are theologically in error."	"I have freedom to eat meat for the glory of God, but I still welcome Christians who disagree."	"I have become all things to all people, that by all means I might save some." (1 Cor. 9:22b)	"I abstain from eating meat for the glory of God, but I still welcome Christians who disagree."	"It's sinful to eat meat, and Christians who do so are being unfaithful to God."	"You must follow the Old Testament dietary restrictions if you want to be a Christian."
HERESY	ARROGANCE	LOVE	LOVE	LOVE	JUDGMENTALISM	HERESY
Distorts the gospel by lawless subtraction	Diminishes the gospel	Reveals the gospel	Magnifies the gospel	Reveals the gospel	Diminishes the gospel	Distorts the gospel by legalistic addition

The goal of every mature believer (three center columns)

WELCOME ONE ANOTHER AS CHRIST HAS WELCOMED US.
ROMANS 15:1-7

Table 6. Paul's solution of love (three center columns)

Here's the gist of what Paul told those with a strong conscience (column 1): "You can continue to use your freedom because in principle you're right about these issues. But what you must not do is look down on (i.e., despise) the strict. You must *welcome* them, learn how to get along with them, and learn to appreciate their subculture. You need to assume that they're being strict for God's glory, not because they're neurotic fundamentalists. And one more thing: when you use your freedoms, don't flaunt them. Don't be 'in-your-face.' That's not showing love. Most important, if the way you use your freedom emboldens a wavering brother or sister to sin against their conscience, you are sinning against that fellow believer. The kingdom of God is so much more than your right to eat and drink certain things."

What was Paul's message to the weak of conscience (summarized in column 3)? "If your strictness in these matters is causing you to judge others and bring division to the church, you are sinning and failing to show love. The kingdom of God is about love and righteousness and peace and joy, not about food (14:17). And one more thing: stop trying to force others to obey the rules of your conscience. Your conscience is for you, not them. Welcome those who disagree with you on food and drink and holy days. Learn about them. Appreciate their robust conscience. Assume that they are exercising their freedoms for God's glory. The kingdom of God is so much more than your scruples about food and holy days."

But the center column (column 2) is the goal of every mature believer. This column reflects the example of Christ and Paul, and it summarizes the message of the first half of Romans 15 as well as 1 Corinthians 9 (not to mention the subject of the present chapter of this book). Our ultimate goal is not simply to stop judging those who are free or to stop looking down on those who are strict. Our ultimate goal is to follow the example of our Lord Jesus, who gave up his rights for others. He joyfully renounced his unbelievable freedom in heaven to come to earth and become an obedient Jew in order to save his people (Rom. 15:3–9).

Likewise, even though Paul agreed with the free group that all food and drink is allowable for a believer (Rom. 14:14, 20), he was so filled with Christ's welcoming love that he happily (not grudgingly) gave up any personal preference if that might result in peace *within* the church or success in winning people *outside* the church to Christ. Around Jews he was happy to be strict. Around Greeks he was happy to be free. He didn't count his freedoms or his comfort as the highest priority but always asked himself these two questions: (1) How does this particular action affect other believers? and (2) How does this particular action further the gospel of Christ? "Paul's overriding concern in this passage," Moo observes, "is not with who is right and who is wrong. He is concerned about unity."[8]

With this fairly complicated but necessary background, let's listen to God instruct us how to disagree with other Christians about disputable matters. The stakes are high; we must understand and internalize these principles if we are to have any hope of unity and joy in our churches.

Twelve Principles about How to Disagree with Other Christians on Disputable Matters[9]

1. Welcome those who disagree with you (Rom. 14:1–2).

As for the one who is weak in faith, welcome him, but not to quarrel over opinions [NIV: "without quarreling over disputable matters"]. One person believes he may eat anything, while the weak person eats only vegetables.

---

[8] Moo, *Encountering the Book of Romans*, 180.
[9] This section revises portions of J. D. Crowley, *Commentary on the Book of Romans for Cambodia and Asia*, ASEAN Bible Commentary (Phnom Penh, Cambodia: Fount of Wisdom, 2014), 227–43, which we have used by permission of the publisher.

Concerning any area of disagreement on third-level matters, a church will have two groups: (1) those who are "weak in faith" (14:1) on that issue and (2) those "who are strong" (15:1). The weak in faith have a weak conscience on that matter, and the strong in faith, a strong conscience. Don't forget that "faith" here refers not to saving faith in Christ (14:22a makes that clear) but to the confidence a person has in their heart or conscience to do a particular activity, such as eat meat (14:2). The weak person's conscience lacks sufficient confidence (i.e., faith) to do a particular act without self-judgment, even if that act is actually not a sin. To him it would be a sin. "The issue is not who has the most faith," Moo notes. "The issue is who thinks that his or her faith lets him or her do this or that."[10] Think once again of the apostle Peter when God commanded him to eat food that his conscience would not allow him to eat (Acts 10:9–16). No one would claim that Peter was weak in *saving* faith; he might have been the strongest Christian alive at the time. But concerning eating unclean meat and hanging out with Gentiles, his faith was very weak indeed. His conscience lacked the confidence (faith) to do those things without self-condemnation.

We are not saying that the faith to eat and faith in Christ are completely unrelated. We believe that the more you understand what faith in Christ means, the more you will be set free from unnecessary regulations in your life. But we must stress again that those with a strong conscience do not necessarily please

---

[10] Moo, *Encountering the Book of Romans*, 181. D. A. Carson and John D. Woodbridge also observe, "Paul holds that a conscience is 'weak' if it makes one think something is wrong when in fact that thing is not itself objectively wrong, wrong in God's eyes." *Letters Along the Way: A Novel of the Christian Life* (Wheaton, IL: Crossway, 1993), 91. Elsewhere, D. A. Carson notes: "The 'weak' brother in this chapter ([1 Cor.] 8:7–13) is one with a 'weak' conscience; that is, one who thinks some action is wrong even though there is nothing intrinsically wrong in it. Thus the 'weak' brother is more bound by rules than the 'strong' brother. Both will adopt the rules that touch things truly wrong, while the weak brother adds rules for things that are not truly wrong but that are at that point wrong for him, since he thinks them wrong." *For the Love of God: A Daily Companion for Discovering the Riches of God's Word* (Wheaton, IL: Crossway, 1998), vol. 1, Sept. 3 entry.

God any more than those with a weak conscience. Both can glorify God, and both can sin against God.

As you are thinking about these issues, perhaps you've already put yourself in a "strong conscience" or "weak conscience" box (though we hardly ever meet a believer willing to admit that they are weak!). But in most issues, you are probably both weak and strong at the same time *in comparison to other people.*[11] Think of a spectrum: there is almost always someone to your left and right on any given disputable issue. For example, if you're the person in figure 5 below who is free to eat meat sold in the meat market without feeling any need to ask questions, Paul says you have a responsibility to resist the temptation to judge the person freer than you to your left *and* a responsibility to resist the temptation to look down on the person stricter than you to the right.

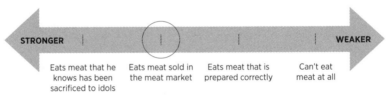

Figure 5. The spectrum of conscience

Not only are there Christians to your left and right, but within your own conscience you might be quite confident and strong to participate in one activity but completely unable to participate in another without self-condemnation. The Christians in Rome were weak or strong with reference to the three specific issues Paul addressed (meat, holy days, and wine), and the weak were strict in all three of those areas. But it's not at all

---

[11] Cf. Robert Duncan Culver, who observes, "Weak consciences abound in every corner of Christendom and perhaps in some corner of every Christian soul." *Systematic Theology: Biblical and Historical* (Fearn, Scotland: Mentor, 2005), 267.

unusual for a person to have a strong conscience on some issues and a weak conscience on others (or, more accurately, stronger on some and weaker on others). The designations *weak conscience* and *strong conscience* apply not to groups of persons across the board but to how each individual approaches specific issues.

A person of my parent's generation told me (J. D.) that she had one college roommate whose conscience would allow her to play with playing cards but not dominos and another roommate who could enjoy dominos but not playing cards. Needless to say, it was a dull year in the dorm!

What this means is that you are responsible to obey *both* Paul's exhortations to the weak and his exhortations to the strong, since (1) there are usually people on either side of you on any given issue and (2) you yourself likely have a stronger conscience on some issues and a weaker conscience on others. This brings us to Paul's second principle when Christians disagree on scruples.

2. Those who have freedom of conscience must not look down on those who don't (Rom. 14:3–4).

> Let not the one who eats despise [NIV: "treat with contempt"] the one who abstains, and let not the one who abstains pass judgment on [i.e., be judgmental toward] the one who eats, for God has welcomed him. Who are you to pass judgment on the servant of another? It is before his own master that he stands or falls. And he will be upheld, for the Lord is able to make him stand.

The strong, who have freedom to do what others cannot do, are tempted to look down on and despise those who are more strict. They may say, "Those people don't understand the freedom we have in Christ. They're not mature like us! They're legalistic. All they think about are rules." Paul condemns this attitude of superiority.

In regard to looking down on others, we must also be careful not to assume that Christians who abstain from a particular activity are doing so out of a weak conscience. For example, perhaps you were part of a subculture that held relatively strict standards on third-level issues, as both of us were. Many people from our background have weak consciences on several third-level issues, but it's a mistake to assume that they all do. Some people in those subcultures have strong consciences on many issues but intentionally refrain from exercising their liberty in order to edify those around them. They contextualize in order to serve others. So avoid assuming that *everyone* in a particular subculture has weaker consciences on certain issues; that's probably not the case.

3. Those whose conscience restricts them must not be judgmental toward those who have freedom (Rom. 14:3–4).
Those who have a weaker conscience on a particular issue are always tempted to pass judgment on those who are freer. They may say, "How can those people be Christians and do that? Don't they know they're hurting the testimony of Christ? Don't they know that they are supposed to give up things like that for the sake of the gospel?"

Paul gives two reasons that it's such a serious sin to break these two principles, that is, for the strong to look down on those with a weaker conscience and for the weak to judge those with a stronger conscience:

1. "God has welcomed him" (14:3c). Do you have the right to reject someone whom God has welcomed? Are you holier than God? If God himself allows his people to hold different opinions on third-level matters, should you force everyone to agree with you?

2. "Who are you to pass judgment on the servant of another?" (14:4a). You are not the master of other believers. When you look down on someone with a weaker conscience or judge someone with a stronger conscience, you're acting as though that person is your servant and you are his master. But God is his master. In matters of opinion, you must let God do his work. You just need to welcome your brother or sister. God is a better master than you are.

We should qualify again that third-level issues are not necessarily unimportant. We don't mean to trivialize them. It's okay to talk about them. It's okay to preach about them. It's okay to tweet and blog about them. It's okay to mention them on Facebook. But with at least two conditions:

1. *Have the right spirit.* Don't be judgmental toward others who are either more or less strict than you. "Do not adopt a critical spirit, a condemning attitude," to quote D. A. Carson.[12] As a general rule, be strict with yourself and generous with others.
2. *Have the right proportion.* Keep disputable matters in their place as third-level issues. Don't treat them like first- or second-level issues. And don't become preoccupied with them or divisive about them. They shouldn't be so important to you that it's all you want to talk about. They shouldn't be the *main* reason that you choose what church to join. They shouldn't be issues that you are the most passionate about such that you are constantly trying to win people over to your position and then looking down on them if they decide not to join your side.

---

[12] D. A. Carson, *Jesus' Sermon on the Mount and His Confrontation with the World: An Exposition of Matthew 5–10* (Grand Rapids, MI: Baker, 1987), 105.

People enjoy being with people like them. But sometimes a subculture can develop within a church in which the majority of people hold particular views on a group of third-level issues. Then when someone joins that assembly, whether coming from another church background or showing up as a new believer, they may feel pressure to embrace the whole package if they want to be a "good" Christian. Also, those in the church who don't hold the views of the majority may feel judged and pressured to change for the wrong reasons.

The stakes get even higher when leaders begin to impose prohibitions that Scripture clearly allows, as did the false teachers Paul warned about in 1 Timothy 4:1–4. Reflecting on that passage and the problem of man-made prohibitions, the Swiss Reformer Ulrich Zwingli echoed Paul when he nailed the source of such ascetic legalism: "Those that take from Christians such freedom by their prohibition are inspired by the devil."[13] This is why the same Paul who urged the strong to "bear with the failings of the weak, and not to please [yourselves]" (Rom. 15:1) told the Colossian Christians something quite different: "Let no one pass judgment on you in questions of food and drink, or with regard to a festival or a new moon or a Sabbath" (Col. 2:16). Paul told them to stand up to those false teachers who wanted to control everyone's consciences, just as he stood up to the false brothers in Jerusalem who wanted to force him to circumcise Titus. The same Paul who said to the Romans, "pursue what makes for peace" (Rom. 14:19), said concerning the circumcision group, "we did not yield in submission even for a moment, so that the truth of the gospel might be preserved for you" (Gal. 2:5). In Antioch, when even Peter wilted under the pressure of the Pork Police from Jerusalem, Paul "opposed

---

[13] Ulrich Zwingli, "Concerning Choice and Liberty Respecting Food—Concerning Offence and Vexation—Whether Anyone Has Power to Forbid Foods at Certain Times—Opinion of Huldreich Zwingli (April 16, 1522)," in *Ulrich Zwingli, Early Writings*, ed. Samuel Macauley Jackson (1912; repr., Durham, NC: The Labyrinth Press, 1987), 76–77.

him to his face" because he knew that the gospel was at stake (Gal. 2:11–14).

You need God's wisdom to discern the difference between (1) weak and wavering believers for whom you must flex and (2) controlling Christians who want to force their scruples on everyone else. Why? So that you, like Paul, can preserve the truth of the gospel for the next generation.

4. Each believer must be fully convinced of their position in their own conscience (Rom. 14:5).

One person esteems one day as better than another, while another esteems all days alike. Each one should be fully convinced in his own mind.

Should Christians celebrate Jewish holy days? This issue, which Paul is addressing here, illustrates the principle that on disputable matters, you should obey your conscience.

This does not mean that your conscience is always right. It's wise to calibrate your conscience to better fit God's will, as we discussed at length in chapter 4. But it does mean that you cannot constantly sin against your conscience and be a healthy Christian. You must be fully convinced of your present position on food or drink or special days—or whatever the issue—and then live consistently by that decision until God may lead you by his Word and Spirit to adjust your conscience.

As we said earlier, the word *conscience* doesn't appear in Romans 14, but the parallel concept of a confident heart on the one hand, and a doubting, accusing heart on the other, is in nearly every verse. And *conscience* occurs eight times in the parallel passage of 1 Corinthians 8 and 10. It's clear from these passages that the consciences of Christians are not identical. And God doesn't expect them to be, or he wouldn't have led Paul to write Romans 14.

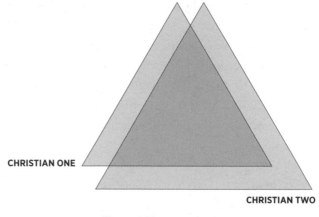

Figure 6. Two consciences

In figure 6 we return to our use of triangles to illustrate that no two Christians have exactly the same conscience. There will be significant overlap, but they're never identical. The areas of disagreement are at the edges where their consciences don't overlap.

The triangle for Christian Two is larger because it's packed with more rules. He has a stricter (or weaker) conscience than Christian One.

You must respect the consciences of others and not make fun of their rules or freedoms. If you have an opportunity, you can slowly help them train their conscience to be more in line with God's standards, but you must never compel someone to sin against their conscience.

If we could understand God's revealed will completely, it would be immediately obvious to us that none of us has a conscience that matches perfectly with God's standards (see figure 7). Realizing this truth brings a spirit of humility into conscience controversies and opens the door to the Holy Spirit's work of calibrating our own consciences to match God's will better.

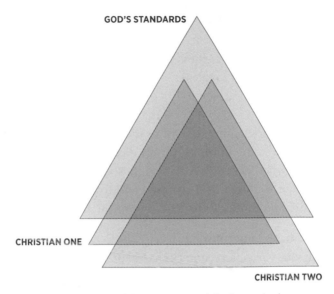

Figure 7. Human conscience and God's standards

As you come to understand God's will more and more, you must do the hard work of continually adding rules to your conscience that God's Word says should be there and continually weeding out rules from your conscience that should not be there. This will take your entire life, but you have the Holy Spirit and the Word of God to help you. God is the only Lord of your conscience.

Paul was a "Pharisee of the Pharisees." When God saved him, his conscience must have been like a bursting suitcase, way overpacked with hundreds of rules, some of which were supposed to be there, but many of which should not have been (for example, his conscience told him to persecute Christians!). It's clear from his later writing that he immediately began the difficult task of tending his conscience for the glory of God, streamlining it until what was left was only what God intended to be there. At least, that was his goal.

*5. Assume that others are partaking or refraining
for the glory of God (Rom. 14:6–9).*

> The one who observes the day, observes it in honor of the
> Lord. The one who eats, eats in honor of the Lord, since he
> gives thanks to God, while the one who abstains, abstains
> in honor of the Lord and gives thanks to God. For none of
> us lives to himself, and none of us dies to himself. For if we
> live, we live to the Lord, and if we die, we die to the Lord.
> So then, whether we live or whether we die, we are the
> Lord's. For to this end Christ died and lived again, that he
> might be Lord both of the dead and of the living.

Notice how generous Paul is to both sides. He assumes
that both sides are exercising their freedoms or restrictions for
the glory of God. Wouldn't it be amazing to be in a church
where everyone gave each other the benefit of the doubt on
these differences, instead of putting the worst possible spin on
everything?

Paul says that both the weak and the strong can please the
Lord even while holding different views on disputable matters.
They have different positions but the same motivation: to honor
God. They both do what they do for the glory of God, not
because they

1. care what others will think or say;
2. want to fit in by being strict like others in their church;
3. want to fit in by exercising freedoms like others in
   their church; or
4. want to break free from their strict background and
   start doing all the stuff they were never allowed to do.

Those are all wrong motivations. And while we should believe
the best about other people and their motives, we shouldn't assume that our motives are okay. In their book *Ethics for a Brave
New World*, John and Paul Feinberg suggest "eight questions

(tests) that each Christian must face when deciding whether or not to indulge in a given activity":[14]

1. Am I fully persuaded that it is right? (Rom. 14:5, 14, 23)
2. Can I do it as unto the Lord? (Rom. 14:6–8)
3. Can I do it without being a stumbling block to my brother or sister in Christ? (Rom. 14:13, 15, 20–22)
4. Does it bring peace? (Rom. 14:17–18)
5. Does it edify my brother? (Rom. 14:19)
6. Is it profitable? (1 Cor. 6:12)
7. Does it enslave me? (1 Cor. 6:12)
8. Does it bring glory to God? (1 Cor. 10:31)

6. Do not judge each other in these matters because we will all someday stand before the judgment seat of God (Rom. 14:10–12).

Why do you pass judgment on your brother? Or you, why do you despise your brother? For we will all stand before the judgment seat of God; for it is written,

> "As I live, says the Lord, every knee shall bow to me,
> and every tongue shall confess to God."

So then each of us will give an account of himself to God.

If we thought more about our own situation before the judgment throne of God, we would be less likely to pass judgment on fellow Christians. On that day we'll be busy enough answering for our own life; we don't need to spend our short life meddling in the lives of others. In these matters where good Christians disagree, we just need to mind our own conscience and let God be the judge of others.

---

[14] John S. Feinberg and Paul D. Feinberg, *Ethics for a Brave New World*, 2nd ed. (Wheaton, IL: Crossway, 2010), 53–55.

7. Your freedom to eat meat is correct, but don't let your freedom destroy the faith of a weak brother (Rom. 14:13–15).

> Therefore let us not pass judgment on one another any longer, but rather decide never to put a stumbling block or hindrance in the way of a brother. I know and am persuaded in the Lord Jesus that nothing is unclean in itself, but it is unclean for anyone who thinks it unclean. For if your brother is grieved by what you eat, you are no longer walking in love. By what you eat, do not destroy the one for whom Christ died.

Free and strict Christians in a church both have responsibilities toward each other. Strict Christians have a responsibility not to impose their conscience on everyone else in the church. It is a serious sin to try to bind someone else's conscience with rules that God does not clearly command.

But the second half of Romans 14 places the bulk of responsibility on Christians with a strong conscience. One obvious reason is that they are strong, so God calls on them to bear with the weaknesses of the weak (Rom. 15:1). Not only that, of the two groups, only the strong have a choice in third-level matters like meat, holy days, and wine. They can either partake or abstain, whereas the conscience of the strict allows them only one choice. It is a great privilege for the strong to have *double* the choices of the weak. They must use this gift wisely by considering how their actions affect the sensitive consciences of their brothers and sisters.

Another reason that the bulk of responsibility falls on the strong has to do with the nature of conscience. As we explain in chapter 3, one of the two great principles of human conscience is "obey it." To disobey conscience can actually jeopardize one's eternal destiny (1 Tim. 1:19). This truth leads Paul to spend the bulk of Romans 14 (and half of 1 Corinthians 8) on the stumbling-block principle: Christians with a strong conscience must not allow their freedom to embolden a weaker brother or sister to sin against their conscience.

The concern here is not merely that your freedom may irritate, annoy, or offend your weaker brother or sister. If a brother or sister simply doesn't like your freedoms, that is their problem. But if your practice of freedom leads your brother or sister to sin against their conscience, then it becomes your problem. Christ gave up his life for that brother or sister; are you unwilling to give up your freedom if that would help your fellow believer avoid sinning against conscience? That's what this passage is talking about when it refers to putting "a stumbling block or hindrance" (Rom. 14:13) in another's way. We shouldn't bring spiritual harm to others (see also vv. 20–21).

So how might your use of freedom bring spiritual harm to other professing believers? Paul isn't clear here, but Doug Moo suggests "two main possibilities":

> [1] Our engaging in an activity that another believer thinks to be wrong may encourage that other believer to do it as well. They would then be sinning because they are not acting "from faith" (v. 23). . . .
>
> [2] An ostentatious flaunting of liberty on a particular matter may so deeply offend someone that he or she may turn from the faith altogether.[15]

Once again we must emphasize that the stumbling block principle does not teach that we must refrain from an activity

---

[15] Moo, *Romans*, 468. Cf. Thomas R. Schreiner, *Romans*, Baker Exegetical Commentary on the New Testament (Grand Rapids, MI: Baker, 1998), 736: "Being 'grieved' [in v. 19] is often understood to denote the feelings of sadness one experiences when others engage in behavior that is deemed inappropriate. . . . [But] the grief intended here relates to eternal destruction. Thus the 'weak' are grieved (or stumble, etc.) if they imitate the behavior of the 'strong' without having the same faith as the 'strong.' What damages the 'weak,' then, is to engage in behavior that is contrary to their faith and conscience. . . . In most modern debates about these and similar issues there is no danger that the more 'traditional' or 'conservative' person will proceed to imitate the behavior of the so-called strong and thus be plunged to eternal ruin." See also Murray, "The Weak and the Strong," 147–48.

that another believer may simply disagree with. For example, the two of us use modern Bible translations such as the ESV and the NIV rather than the KJV because the Scripture writers wrote in the common language of the people. Yet we know Christians who are very unhappy when we use a translation other than the KJV. As best we can see, we are bringing no spiritual harm to them when we use a modern translation; that is, we're not emboldening them to sin against their conscience and put themselves in danger of turning away from Christianity. So we don't need to refrain from using modern translations for their sake; doing so poses no stumbling block. That said, Christian love and flexibility may lead us to use the KJV in certain situations.

Moo highlights another common misunderstanding about the stumbling-block principle:

> In Christian books and from Christian pulpits one sometimes hears Romans 14 applied something like this: believers should refrain from drinking alcohol out of deference to other Christians who might be inclined to overindulge and abuse alcohol. Those other Christians are the "weaker brothers and sisters"—weak because they have a weakness for alcohol. The principle, of course, is valid enough. Christians should recognize the weaknesses of fellow Christians and do what they can to keep them from succumbing to those weaknesses. But we must point out that this idea of "weakness" is not what Paul is talking about in Romans 14. The weak brother or sister in this chapter is the one who is weak in faith. They believe that their faith does not allow them to do certain things. The weakness has nothing to do with an emotional or physical susceptibility. It is a theological weakness.[16]

---

[16] Moo, *Encountering the Book of Romans*, 184. See also Murray, "The Weak and the Strong," 136–53.

We must never allow the conscience of others to determine our own conscience. But we must always consider the conscience of others when we determine our own actions.

8. Disagreements about eating and drinking are not important in the kingdom of God; building each other up in righteousness, peace, and joy is the important thing (Rom. 14:16–21).

> So do not let what you regard as good be spoken of as evil. For the kingdom of God is not a matter of eating and drinking but of righteousness and peace and joy in the Holy Spirit. Whoever thus serves Christ is acceptable to God and approved by men. So then let us pursue what makes for peace and for mutual upbuilding.
>
> Do not, for the sake of food, destroy the work of God. Everything is indeed clean, but it is wrong for anyone to make another stumble by what he eats. It is good not to eat meat or drink wine or do anything that causes your brother to stumble.

The New Testament clearly and repeatedly lays down the principle that God is completely indifferent to what we ingest. First and most important, the Lord Jesus himself memorably proclaimed all foods to be legitimate for eating in Mark 7:1–23 (esp. vv. 18–19). Since Peter didn't seem to get the memo, the Lord Jesus had to give him a vision three times to show him that Christians must not make food an issue (Acts 10:9–16). Then in 1 Corinthians 8:8, Paul comes right out and says it: "Food will not commend us to God. We are no worse off if we do not eat, and no better off if we do." And just in case we still didn't get it, God gave us Romans 14:17, which shows that the kingdom of God has nothing to do with food and drink. Nothing. God doesn't care at all about what we ingest.

This might seem mistaken. Doesn't God care if we take poison? Not if the purpose is to cure. Every day Christians take poison into their bodies to cure themselves of cancer. But if we take in poison to kill ourselves, that's another matter entirely. In Christianity, *why* you do things is more important than *what* you do.

There is something striking and truly counterintuitive about Paul's reasoning here and in 1 Corinthians 8:8. Paul appropriates an argument that the strong want to use for their side (that what we eat or drink doesn't matter to God so quit making a big deal about it) to instead *chasten* the strong. Since food and drink do not commend us to God, since the kingdom of God is not about food and drink, since food and drink are not matters of importance, *then why not voluntarily abstain if your freedom could harm the faith of a wavering Christian?* Fortunately, we rarely encounter this decision, but we have to be willing to make it.

Paul mentions just "eating and drinking" in verse 17, but this principle extends to many other disputable matters. The kingdom of God is not a matter of schooling choices, political parties, musical styles, and so on. Once again, we're not suggesting that third-level matters are unimportant. We have some strong opinions on them. But they are not what the kingdom of God is about. The most important thing is not what we eat or drink. Schismatically dividing over these less important matters does not make "for peace and for mutual upbuilding" (Rom. 14:19).[17]

9. If you have freedom, don't flaunt it; if you are strict, don't expect others to be strict like you (Rom. 14:22a).

The faith that you have, keep between yourself and God.

This truth applies equally to the strong and the weak. To those with a strong conscience you have much freedom in

---

[17] Of course, there will always be some Christians who go beyond the limits of these principles and use freedom as an excuse for lawlessness. This is another reason churches need Spirit-filled pastors to shepherd and warn their (sometimes self-deceived) sheep.

Christ. But don't flaunt it or show it off in a way that may cause others to sin. Be especially careful to nurture the faith of young people and new Christians.

Those of you with a weak conscience in a particular area also have a responsibility not to "police" others by pressuring them to adopt your strict standards. You should keep these matters between yourself and God.

As we saw in table 5 above, those who are strict may be prone to an even more serious error, namely, insisting that everyone *must* hold their view in order to be a Christian. When you say that holding a particular view on a disputable matter is essential to be a Christian, you have crossed the line into legalism.[18] Here's how Sam Storms defines legalism: "Legalism is the tendency to regard as divine law things that God has neither required nor forbidden in Scripture, and the corresponding inclination to look with suspicion on others for their failure or refusal to conform. . . . Do you elevate to the status of moral law something the Bible does not require?"[19]

10. A person who lives according to their conscience is blessed (Rom. 14:22b–23).

> Blessed is the one who has no reason to pass judgment on himself for what he approves. But whoever has doubts is condemned if he eats, because the eating is not from faith. For whatever does not proceed from faith is sin.

God gave us the gift of conscience in order to significantly increase our joy as we obey its warnings. As we saw in chapter 1 and explored further in chapter 4, one of the two great principles of conscience is to obey it. "Paul judges it dangerous

---

[18] Cf. Carson and Woodbridge, *Letters Along the Way*, 92; R. C. Sproul, *The Gospel of God: An Exposition of Romans*, Focus on the Bible Commentary (Fearn, Scotland: Christian Focus, 1999), 237.

[19] Sam Storms, *Tough Topics: Biblical Answers to 25 Challenging Questions* (Wheaton, IL: Crossway, 2013), 311.

for Christians to defy their consciences, because if they get in the habit of ignoring the voice of conscience, they may ignore that voice even when the conscience is well informed and properly warning them of something that is positively evil."[20] Just as God's gift of touch and pain guards us from what would rob us of physical health, conscience continually guards us from the sin that robs our joy.

11. We must follow the example of Christ, who put others first (Rom. 15:1–6).

> We who are strong have an obligation to bear with the failings of the weak, and not to please ourselves. Let each of us please his neighbor for his good, to build him up. For Christ did not please himself, but as it is written, "The reproaches of those who reproached you fell on me." For whatever was written in former days was written for our instruction, that through endurance and through the encouragement of the Scriptures we might have hope. May the God of endurance and encouragement grant you to live in such harmony with one another, in accord with Christ Jesus, that together you may with one voice glorify the God and Father of our Lord Jesus Christ.

This principle doesn't mean that the strong have to agree with the position of the weak. It doesn't even mean that the strong can never again exercise their freedoms. On the other hand, neither does it mean that the strong only put up with or endure or tolerate the weak, like a person who tolerates someone who annoys him. For a Christian, to "bear with" the weaknesses of the weak means that you gladly help the weak by refraining from doing anything that would hurt their faith.

Be careful not to misunderstand verse 2: "Let each of us

---

[20] D. A. Carson, *The Cross and Christian Ministry: An Exposition of Passages from 1 Corinthians* (Grand Rapids, MI: Baker, 1993), 123.

please his neighbor." Paul is not telling you to become a "people pleaser" who cares more about what others think than about what God thinks. The choice is not between pleasing people and pleasing God, but between pleasing others and pleasing yourself. Christian freedom is not "I always do what I want." Nor is it "I always do whatever the other person wants." It is "I do what brings glory to God. I do what brings others under the influence of the gospel. I do what leads to peace in the church."

Romans 15:3 emphasizes the example of Christ. We cannot even begin to imagine the freedoms and privileges that belonged to the Son of God in heaven. To be God is to be completely free. Yet Christ "did not please himself" but gave up his rights and freedoms to become a servant so that we could be saved from wrath. Compared to what Christ suffered on the cross, to give up a freedom like eating meat is a trifle indeed.

12. We bring glory to God when we welcome one another as Christ has welcomed us (Rom. 15:7).

Therefore welcome one another as Christ has welcomed you, for the glory of God.

With this sentence, Paul bookends this long section that began with similar words in 14:1: "Welcome him. . . ." But here in 15:7 Paul adds a comparison—"as Christ has welcomed you"—and a purpose—"for the glory of God." It matters how you treat those who disagree with you on disputable matters. When you welcome them as Christ has welcomed you, you glorify God.

Conclusion

This is God's brilliant solution when Christians disagree about disputable matters. It is much easier said than done. So let's ask God for grace to respond to his Word in a way that gives him glory:

Father, we are finite and sinful people, and for a complex of reasons that you know far better than we do, we disagree with our fellow brothers and sisters in Christ on all sorts of disputable matters.

1. *Would you please give us grace to welcome those who disagree with us on various disputable issues?*
2. *Would you please give us grace to not look down on those who are stricter than we are?*
3. *Would you please give us grace to not be judgmental toward those who exercise more freedom than we do?*
4. *Would you please give us grace to be fully convinced of our positions in our own consciences?*
5. *Would you please give us grace to practice our freedoms and restrictions for your glory and to assume that other believers are doing the same?*
6. *Would you please give us grace to keep disputable matters in perspective, knowing that we will all someday stand before your judgment seat?*
7. *Would you please give us grace to not let our freedom destroy the faith of a professing Christian who is weaker on a particular disputable matter?*
8. *Would you please give us grace to build each other up in righteousness, peace, and joy?*
9. *Would you please give us grace to not flaunt our freedom or expect others to be as strict as we are?*
10. *Would you please give us grace to live according to our conscience and experience your blessing?*
11. *Would you please give us grace to follow the example of Christ, who put others first?*
12. *Would you please give us grace to bring you glory by welcoming one another as Christ has welcomed us?*

Lord, we are weak and selfish. We need so much endurance and encouragement to live with our brothers and sisters in this way of peace. You are the God of endurance and encouragement. Please grant us to live in such harmony with one another and in accord with Christ Jesus that together we may with one voice glorify you, the God and Father of our Lord Jesus Christ. Amen.

6

HOW SHOULD YOU RELATE TO PEOPLE IN OTHER CULTURES WHEN YOUR CONSCIENCES DISAGREE?

If conscience issues are so complex within your own culture, can you imagine how complicated things get when you *cross* cultures? Yet every year church planters start churches on the other side of town and missionaries go to the other side of the world with little or no understanding of what's in their own conscience, let alone the conscience of the people they are going to serve. It doesn't even cross their minds, for example, that their own standards of privacy and private property rights may be quite different from those in the new location.

Do They Even *Have* a Conscience?

I (J. D.) planted a mango tree in my yard in Cambodia. On the fourth year, when fruit normally starts to appear, it produced a grand total of three mangoes, and they were pretty pitiful. But that couldn't dampen my excitement for the day when I could slice off some of that golden goodness and savor my very own homegrown mango. The day never came. A local friend of mine who was doing some concrete work for me picked and ate the mangoes. All three of them! Worse yet, he seemed completely without remorse—a sign, I was sure, of a seared conscience.

But there was a less sinister explanation. He felt no pangs of conscience because in his culture, what he did wasn't wrong. The real wrong in that situation was my stinginess. In most cultures around the world (including ancient Israel, by the way—see Deut. 23:24–25 and Luke 6:1), it's not considered theft to pick a handful of grain or a fruit or two while you're taking a shortcut through someone's field as long as you don't do any serious harvesting. For most Western missionaries though, that would constitute *two* violations of personal property: trespass and theft. Both my culture and the Cambodian culture have strong moral codes against theft, but the difference is in the details.

As I said, the real scandal of that event was my stinginess, not my friend's "theft," as I perceived it. At that point, I realized that I had to make two calibrations to my inner moral compass. First, I had to add the category of "stinginess toward neighbors" to my list of serious wrongs. Stinginess toward neighbors is hardly on the radar in the U.S., where people revere personal property rights and think they're quoting Scripture when they say, "God helps those who help themselves." But in most other cultures, it is a cardinal sin. Food is above all what we must share with others.[1]

Second, I had to adjust my conscience concerning personal property rights. Later, while walking through an orchard in Cambodia, a friend handed me some freshly picked fruit. Because I had calibrated my conscience, I felt completely free to

---

[1] Robert J. Priest, "Missionary Elenctics: Conscience and Culture," *Missiology: An International Review* 22, no. 3 (1994): 297; Priest, "Cultural Factors in Victorious Living," in *Free and Fulfilled: Victorious Living in the 21st Century*, ed. Robertson McQuilkin (Nashville, TN: Nelson, 1997), 128–42.

eat it even though we had not yet asked the owner. (Of course, these rules have stipulations. If we had climbed a wall to get the fruit, it would have been theft. And I have to remember to recalibrate when I go back to the States, where I can get arrested for picking a piece of fruit!)

If we diagram the above situation using the conscience triangles from chapter 1, it might look like what we see in figure 8:

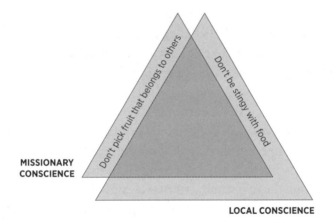

Figure 8. Missionary conscience and local conscience

Each of us tended to see the "sin" for which the other person had no conscience category.[2] Since "Don't pick fruit that belongs to others" was a big part of my conscience, I immediately saw my friend's "brazen" disregard for that obvious command. Since "Don't be stingy with food" was a big part of my friend's conscience, he immediately saw my obvious moral failure.

An Ally Goes Silent

It doesn't take much imagination to see how messy things can get when Christians who are ignorant of both their own

---

[2] Priest, "Missionary Elenctics," 297.

conscience and the moral judgments of the other culture begin proclaiming repentance of sins and faith in Christ. Whose sins? What sins?

What if I tried to use the "theft" of my three mangoes to show my friend the depravity of his heart and his need for Christ? My pleas would have fallen on a deaf conscience. Normally conscience is a powerful and indispensable ally in evangelism as we urge people to repent of sin and turn to Christ. But we must be careful what specific sins we ask them to repent of. There are three dangers here.

1. There is a danger that we'll preach against sins that are not truly sins in any culture, but simply cultural accretions, baggage that we've carried to our new country from the West or, worse yet, from our Christian subculture. "Doth not nature itself teach you that it is a sin to use certain instruments in worship or to destroy forests with slash-and-burn agriculture or to put your ten-year-old child to work in your field or to be late for a church service?" When we preach against those kinds of "sins," the conscience of our hearers won't affirm our message. It remains completely silent.

True, with enough persuasion and force of Western personality, we can convince the puzzled locals that the issues we keep bringing up are actually important, but it won't be the Holy Spirit using the holy Word to do the convincing. The result? Another group of Christians with overburdened consciences. And remember that an overburdened conscience is a conscience ripe for error. When you, through your influence, make enough small things into big things in the hearts of the local believers, you will only be setting them up to overlook something huge that will truly harm their life and family. If they learn to strain out enough gnats, they'll eventually choke to death on a camel.

2. There is a danger that we'll preach against what those of

us in the West consider a true sin but those in the local culture do not because we define the details of the command differently. Such was the case when my friend picked fruit in my field. Once again, the chirping of crickets will replace the magisterial judgments of conscience, all because the messengers didn't bother to understand either their own moral standards or the moral standards of the locals.

3. There is a danger that we'll not be careful to value the virtues of the local people's conscience. When we break cultural values that the other culture embraces as important but our own culture considers inconsequential—such as sharing food or honoring the elderly or dressing appropriately—people in that culture will see us as immoral. The locals will look down on both us and our message.

If you want the hearer's conscience to powerfully affirm your gospel witness, you must (1) preach repentance from sins that are clearly sins in both the Bible and the consciences of the people in the target culture and (2) cultivate those virtues of the target culture's conscience that are not traditionally a part of yours. These principles apply especially to the early stages of evangelism.[3]

Because God created us in his image, we can expect all cultures to have good, wholesome values and traditions that we can wholeheartedly affirm and learn from. But because humans are also fallen, we can expect all cultures to have values and traditions that displease God. Wise missionaries study both their own culture and the target culture to find these wholesome

---

[3] Priest, "Missionary Elenctics," 309. Limiting your preaching to only those sins that show up in the native conscience is not a hard and fast rule. For example, I (J. D.) have found it helpful in my evangelism both in Asia and the States to *add* a category of sin to the hearers' conscience that was never there before: the sin of knowing that a Creator God exists but not acknowledging him or giving him thanks (Rom. 1:21–23). This is the ultimate sin, the primordial sin: wanting God's things but not the God who made those things. I've seen the Holy Spirit prick the conscience of people who had never thought about this as a sin. The Holy Spirit can do quick work in a human conscience when we preach repentance from *real* sins and faith in the Lord Jesus.

and unwholesome aspects so that they and their converts can embrace the good and turn from the evil.

The Unexamined Conscience of a Missionary

A missionary with an unexamined, uncalibrated conscience will hardly ever think in these terms. As we have already emphasized, no two Christians have exactly the same conscience, though there is much overlap. If two Christians in the West have such divergence at the edges of conscience, imagine the differences between a Western missionary and an unbeliever from the global South. The challenges multiply across cultures:

> Western missionaries tended to assume that their consciences were advanced beyond that of local peoples, who they felt had little if any sense of right and wrong. They took on themselves the task of teaching moral scruples, all too often imposing new cultural (rather than biblical) values and belittling or trampling on local values in the process.
>
> To understand the cultural forms of conscience is of critical importance in missionary work. It carries implications for elenctics (the conviction of sin) as well as cross-cultural ethics. When we feel that another does not have a proper conscience, we are tempted to develop one that matches ours. When we develop ethical systems, they tend to blend our cultural values together with biblical values, and may not make sense to our target population.[4]

We're not aware of anyone who has thought more deeply about the nexus of conscience, culture, and missions than Bob Priest, Professor of International Studies, Mission, and Anthropology at Trinity Evangelical Divinity School. Raised in Bolivia, he later conducted nearly two years of anthropological field

---

[4] A. Scott Moreau, "Conscience," in *Evangelical Dictionary of World Missions*, ed. A. Scott Moreau, Baker Reference Library (Grand Rapids, MI: Baker, 2000), 224.

research among the Aguaruna of Peru, focusing on traditional religion and conversion to Christianity. He has written two strikingly insightful articles on the issue of conscience, and this chapter borrows much from his insights.[5]

Priest shares the critical insight that "in an intercultural situation each interactant will . . . tend to condemn the other morally for behavior about which the other has no conscience":

> A North American going to live with the Aguaruna may be highly incensed at the occasional beating of an errant wife, at arranged marriages, at polygyny, or at the marriages of 13-year-old girls to 45-year-old men. For traditional Aguaruna each of these is perfectly wholesome and appropriate. On the other hand, the Aguaruna are angered when North American anthropologists or missionaries fail to share the food they are eating with visitors. Food is, above all things, that which must be shared. And when such foreigners are invited for a meal, they fail to exercise careful self-restraint in eating meat—a limited and highly valued food item. Self-restraint, in such a setting, implies consideration for the needs of others and self-denial on their behalf.[6]

Priest is not suggesting that wife-beating and polygyny are disputable matters. He highlights them in order to show that both missionaries and locals are often oblivious to behavior that doesn't violate their own conscience.

Priest also describes how cultural conscience standards differ on modesty:

> Cultures vary in what is thought of as erotic, and thus in what modesty entails. For many medieval Europeans a woman's bare feet were thought highly erotic, while the bosom was associated primarily with nursing. . . . Similarly,

---

[5] Priest, "Missionary Elenctics"; Priest, "Cultural Factors."
[6] Priest, "Missionary Elenctics," 297.

contemporary Fulani men say it is the sight of a woman's thighs that stimulates lustful desires. They find it hilarious that Western women go swimming in suits that carefully cover the bosom, a matter of relative indifference to modesty, while flagrantly uncovering their thighs to the world. . . . For many Arab men, on the other hand, the mere sight of a woman's hair tends to stimulate lustful thoughts. Modest Arab women cover their hair in public. Behavior and dress that are appropriately modest in one cultural context may be deemed shockingly immodest in another context. Christian modesty in the U.S. will look quite different from Christian modesty in Iran.[7]

In another example, Priest explains that

American missionaries internalize deeply held moral ideas about punctuality, egalitarianism, individual rights, privacy, cleanliness, etc., which derive much more clearly from their culture than from the Scriptures.[8]

These cultural differences in convictions show why it's so important to understand what the conscience is and how it works:

For us to train our missionaries in Bible schools which stress modesty by specific rules addressing the permissible length

---

[7] Priest, "Cultural Factors," 135–36. "Behavior is, after all, what missionaries see. Conscience is what they see with. What they do not see, because it is internal and not directly visible, is the conscience of the other person. Thus the case of a missionary in an African village who 'saw immodesty' in the form of uncovered breasts. What she saw with, and took for granted, was her own conscience. What she failed to see was native conscience. Thus she failed to see what was really relevant which was that modest women cover, not their breasts, but their legs so that men not lust. In failing to see their conscience, she failed to understand that these people 'saw immodesty' when they looked at her bare legs. For it was through the lens of their own conscience that they saw her." "Missionary Elenctics," 297.

Priest's comment about Iran may raise a more difficult question: Is the modesty that the Iranian culture demands of women sinful (i.e., beyond third-level, disputable matters)? Is cultural modesty in Iran so intertwined with Sharia law that to conform to cultural norms may enable sin? That is, is it a culturally inculcated sin? It's possible that the rules are so oppressive that to not teach against them would be sin, but because we have limited knowledge as external observers, it appears that only a native insider could make this call.

[8] Priest, "Missionary Elenctics," 300.

of skirts (measured in terms of inches above the knee), for example, and then to send such missionaries out to radically different cultures (from tribals in grass skirts and uncovered breasts to Muslims with carefully veiled women) and expect them to figure out, on their own, the precise mix of culture and Scripture which has gone into their deeply held convictions of conscience about modesty is an unrealistic expectation.[9]

Bob Priest argues that if missionaries fail to treat cross-cultural conscience issues with care, they may bypass the native conscience, and natives may "convert" not to Christianity but to a different culture. Some may do this because they hope "by a cultural conversion to acquire the secrets of wealth and power." So it's essential that missionaries "understand the role that culture has played in the formation of their own conscience" and that they "understand native conscience." Priest recommends that if a missionary wants to reach people in other cultures, he or she should (1) "seek to live an exemplary life in terms of the virtues and norms stressed by the people he or she is attempting to reach" and (2) "should stress sin, guilt, and repentance principally with reference to native conscience—*particularly that aspect of their conscience which is in agreement with Scripture.*"[10]

Priest goes into much more detail than we can share here. Our point in sharing these highlights is that it's important to understand what the conscience is because that helps you evangelize and edify others in different cultures.

Calibrating Your Conscience for Missions

Perhaps the best example in the Bible of a person who did the hard work of weeding and cultivating his conscience for the

---

[9] Ibid., 301.
[10] Ibid., 304, 306, 308, 309.

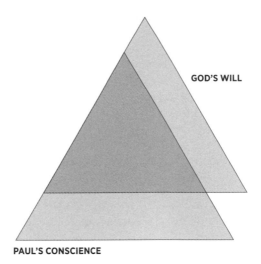

GOD'S WILL

PAUL'S CONSCIENCE

Figure 9. The overlap of God's standards and Paul's conscience

sake of winning people to Christ is the apostle Paul. Think about what a tangled jungle the overly sensitive conscience of a scrupulous Pharisee like Paul must have been, with the addition of hundreds of man-made laws that weren't in the Scripture!

Remember that no Christian's conscience perfectly aligns with God's will. The same was true for Paul on the day of his conversion. Many of the rules in his conscience matched God's will (the overlap in figure 9), but many did not (the lower part of Paul's triangle in figure 9). Not only that, no doubt some commandments of God didn't yet show up in Paul's conscience (the nonoverlapping section to the top right in figure 9).

Like Paul's conscience, the conscience of every believer is a mixture of rules that are informed by God's will (the upper part of Paul's conscience in figure 10) and rules that are merely cultural or personal (the lower part in figure 10).

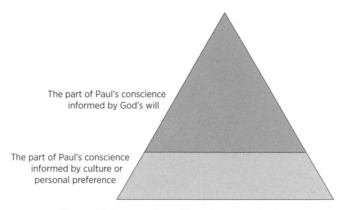

Figure 10. Two sources of conscience standards

Don't you wish that the line between the two were as obvious as it is in figure 10? But in real life, it's much more difficult to know where God's moral judgments end and your own begin, as figure 11 shows. This fuzzy line makes the task of calibrating conscience much more difficult.

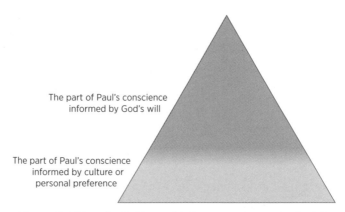

Figure 11. Where do God's moral judgments end and mine begin?

What Stays? What Goes? What's Missing?

It's clear from Paul's later cultural flexibility that at some point in his life, he prayed something like this: "God, it's time for you to weed the garden. It's time for me to bring my conscience under your lordship. I'm no longer the lord of my conscience. God, show me the laws that are missing from my conscience and the man-made weeds I need to uproot." So one by one, he started making decisions about what stayed and what went—what was truly a matter of right and wrong and what was more a matter of preference or opinion. He asked three questions: Lord, what stays, what goes, and what's missing?

The prohibition against eating pork? Jesus said in Mark 7 that such a prohibition was no longer a matter of right and wrong. It was just a preference. Do you think it was easy for Paul to make that switch? We're sure it wasn't, but Paul still obeyed. You can teach your conscience.

Special Jewish holy days? "Out they go. Whether I observe holy days or not, it's no longer a conscience issue but a matter of wisdom, love, and gospel witness."

Love for enemies? That was probably missing from Paul's conscience! He had to add it.

Special kosher hand-washing rituals? "Get out of my conscience. But if I'm invited to the synagogue leader's house for a meal, I might do the ceremonial hand washing out of love for him and sensitivity to his conscience."

Paul kept doing that until his conscience contained only—and all of—those rules that God intended to be there, matters that were truly right and wrong from God's perspective (at least, that was Paul's goal). He separated conscience issues from matters of preference or culture or manners or hygiene.

So what did he do with all the rules that he removed from his conscience? Was it party time for Paul? Ham, stuffed with crab, wrapped in bacon every day? Of course not. It was never about Paul. It was never about food. It was about Jesus and the gospel. The matters that he weeded from his conscience were now the very matters that he could flex on for the sake of the gospel or for the sake of a weaker Christian. It was in those matters that he became all things to all people for the sake of the gospel. (You don't flex on things that you are convinced are matters of right or wrong. That's called sin.)

Eat pork? If it advances the gospel. Stop eating pork? If it advances the gospel. Celebrate a Jewish holy day? Sure, when I'm in Jerusalem. Abstain from wine or meat sacrificed to idols? No problem, if partaking might embolden my brother with a weak conscience in those areas to sin.

Paul became someone who could glide from culture to culture, making nearly seamless transitions without attracting attention to himself, because it was not about him. It was about Christ and the gospel and the eternal souls of men and women.

How do we know he tended his conscience in this way? Because later this once scrupulous legalist described his cultural flexibility like this:

> For though I am free from all [people and their cultures], I have made myself a servant to all, *that I might win more of them*. To the Jews I became as a Jew, *in order to win Jews*. To those under the law I became as one under the law (though not being myself under the law) *that I might win those under the law*. To those outside the law I became as one outside the law (not being outside the law of God but under the law of Christ) *that I might win those outside the law*. To the weak I became weak, *that I might win the weak*. I have become all things to all people, *that by all means I might save some*. I do it all *for the sake of the gospel*, that I may share with them in its blessings. (1 Cor. 9:19–23)

He was able to do this because he had done the hard work of calibrating his conscience to match God's standards, not the standards of people. And what motivated him to develop this kind of cultural flexibility? He mentions the reason seven times in this paragraph: winning more people for the sake of the gospel (note the italicized words in the preceding quotation).

We, too, must seriously and prayerfully do the difficult work of streamlining our conscience under the direction of the Holy Spirit and his Word. This will mean creating new categories in our minds, new files, to which we will move the matters that we previously placed in the category of "Right and Wrong." One file might say, "Family Rules," another, "Wisdom Issues," another, "Hygiene," another, "Good Manners." I (J. D.) have at least three different "Good Manners" files: one for when I'm in America, one for when I'm among Khmer in Cambodia, and one for when I'm among tribal minorities in Cambodia. All three cultures care very much about appropriate manners, but the details are different.

Christian Liberty: The Freedom to Discipline Yourself to Be Flexible for the Gospel

First Corinthians 9:19–23 presents two general categories of people: (1) people like Paul who become all things to all men for the sake of the gospel and (2) people for whom those like Paul flex. The question for those committed to gospel living is this: how do I go from being the ethnocentric person for whom Paul must flex to being the person like Paul who is doing this amazing flexing while flowing from culture to culture?

It's not easy. It requires years of carefully tending the garden of your conscience. Or to use our original metaphor, it requires years of calibrating and recalibrating your conscience. It requires spiritual maturity, theological conviction, Christian love, personal discipline, and an unswerving commitment to the gospel. It should come as no surprise, then, that the paragraphs before and after 1 Corinthians 9:19–23 are all about self-denial and self-discipline for the sake of the gospel and the sake of the lost.

That's what Christian liberty really is: *the freedom to discipline yourself to be flexible for the sake of the gospel.* This definition comes straight from 1 Corinthians 9:19, as illustrated in table 7:

1 CORINTHIANS 9:19	CHRISTIAN LIBERTY IS . . .
For though I am free from all	the freedom
I have made myself	to discipline myself
a servant to all	to be flexible
that I might win more of them.	for the sake of the gospel.

Table 7. Christian liberty according to 1 Corinthians 9:19

Christian liberty isn't, "Cool! I finally get to do the stuff I've always wanted to do but my strict upbringing wouldn't let me." Then you Facebook about it so that everyone knows you're hip. That's not Christian liberty; that's immaturity. Christian liberty is the domain of the mature, not the immature. When the immature get ahold of it, they make a mess of it, like some of the Corinthians did.

Christian liberty is not about you and your freedom to do what you want to do. It's all about the freedom to discipline yourself to be flexible for the sake of the gospel and for the sake of weaker believers.

Let's flesh out this freedom with some real-life missionary examples:

- Christian liberty is the freedom to eat dog when natives in the village serve it to you.

- Christian liberty is the freedom to choose never again to eat southern BBQ and double bacon cheeseburgers because you're called to serve Christ in the Muslim areas of Detroit.

- Christian liberty is the freedom that comes to a single lady missionary who was brought up to have personal scruples against wearing pants but who disciplines herself to wear the indigenous clothing of a tribe in Central Asia—including pants—because in that culture, only loose women wear dresses and show their ankles and calves.

- Christian liberty is the freedom that allows a very private person to open up her home in a society where people just walk in without knocking, a society that doesn't even have a word for *privacy*. (I [J. D.] just described my wife.)

- Christian liberty is about a clean freak who restrains himself from getting out his hand sanitizer every time he shakes someone's hand or touches something in a third-world country. We heard of a missionary couple who ruined their ministry because of fastidiousness that had wormed its way into their conscience.

- Christian liberty is the freedom to sing and dance to tribal hymns the way *the tribal people* sing and dance to them, even though, by upbringing and personality, you have never been comfortable showing that kind of emotion in worship. (I [J. D.] just described myself.)

- Christian liberty is the freedom for someone who hates bugs to discipline himself to live where bugs nightly invade homes during certain seasons of the year.

- Christian liberty is about a Corinthian Christian getting invited to his unsaved neighbor's house for a feast and being served meat that he doesn't want to eat because of former convictions but eating it anyway for the sake of the gospel—because that man's eternal soul matters a whole lot more than some scruple about not eating meat (1 Cor. 10:27).

- Christian liberty is about another Corinthian Christian at the same party who has no scruples against eating meat. And just as he gets ready to dig into the slab of steak on his plate, someone sitting next to him leans over and says, "Don't eat it; it's been sacrificed." And for the sake of that man and his weak conscience, the meat lover puts down his fork and says, "Thank you for telling me that" (1 Cor. 10:28–29).

That's what Christian liberty is all about: being free to discipline yourself to put the gospel and others first.

I (J. D.) have a missionary colleague who was brought up as a vegetarian. That restriction became entrenched in his conscience to the point that he considered himself morally superior to those with a different diet. After he became a Christian in college, he began to understand the Bible's teaching about food. He remained a vegetarian, but he moved that practice out of the category of right and wrong to the category of preference. He no longer judged others concerning food. As he prepared to become a Bible translator to a tribe in Asia, he realized that this preference would cause problems not only during prefield ministry but especially when he was invited into the homes of local believers on the field. How could he refuse to eat the food offered to him by his tribal brothers and sisters? So he forced himself to learn to eat meat again, and he eats meat to this day. Had he stayed in his own country, he would likely still be a vegetarian. Notice that because he had already done the work of calibrating his conscience on food issues, he was free, then, either to eat meat or to be a vegetarian, depending on what was best for the gospel.

A message to future missionaries: You can't live this kind of life if your conscience is cluttered with all manner of restrictions that God hasn't instituted. If you've taken fifty little issues and made them into big issues in your conscience, those are fifty fewer areas in which you will be able to follow Paul's missionary example of flexing, because if your conscience says those fifty issues are sins, then you can't bend on any of them.

If what you eat and drink is in the category of black and white, you can't flex on that. If pristine hygiene has made its way into your conscience as a matter of right and wrong, you can't flex on that. If what you do with your hands while you worship is a moral absolute, you can't bend on that.

If your conscience tells you that it's wrong to eat animals, there goes your ministry to 90 percent of the people in the world. If you think privacy is next to godliness, you won't last long in most countries. If your conscience won't let you dance to tribal hymns, stay away from Africa. Or just import all Western hymns, and sing them exactly like you do at home—and don't forget to take a piano!

But if you do that, you'll end up with what Professor Mark Vowels calls "franchise missions," little cookie-cutter duplicates of our home church in a foreign country: same dress, same songs, same buildings, and the same bound consciences—bound by things that those poor folks had no idea were even sins until the missionaries came and brought American Christian subculture, *adding* to their burden instead of lifting it.

D. A. Carson reminds us that both the too-careful and the not-careful-enough need to hear this exhortation from 1 Corinthians 9:19–23:

> The person who lives by endless rules and who forms his or her self-identity by conforming to them simply cannot flex at all. By contrast, the person without roots, heritage, self-identity, and nonnegotiable values is not really flexing, but is simply being driven hither and yon by the vagaries of

every whimsical opinion that passes by. Such people may "fit in," but they cannot win anyone. They hold to nothing stable or solid enough to win others to it! Thus the end of Paul's statement in verse 22 is critical: "I have become all things to all men *so that by all possible means I might save some*" (9:22).[11]

The Church: God's Cross-Cultural Laboratory for Missions

Where do you get missionaries like Paul who have done the hard work of tending their conscience and who know how to negotiate these difficult cultural situations without exporting merely cultural Christianity? You grow them. You grow them in the church, which is God's laboratory for learning how to reach other cultures.

The Bible gives clear evidence that God intends the little clashes of culture in your church to get you ready for the really difficult clashes of culture in missions and evangelism. At least, the church is *supposed* to be that laboratory. There are so many Christians in America that we have the luxury of dividing up into smaller and smaller subsets so that we can be part of a church where members hold very few uncomfortable differences of opinion on matters of conscience. We even enshrine some of those scruples in our bylaws to guarantee unity—or, more accurately, uniformity.

Twice in the Bible, Paul deliberately connects (1) the messiness of getting along in church with people who have different consciences with (2) mission to the unreached. One is the famous missions passage we just looked at in 1 Corinthians 9:19–23, in which Paul defends his own practice of cultural flexibility in order to win as many as possible among groups with differing scruples. This famous missionary text comes

---

[11] D. A. Carson, *The Cross and Christian Ministry: An Exposition of Passages from 1 Corinthians* (Grand Rapids, MI: Baker, 1993), 121.

right in the middle of Paul's exhortation to the Corinthian believers to be sensitive to the weak consciences of others in their church (1 Corinthians 8 and 10). Flexibility in church life gets you ready for flexibility in missions.

Even clearer is the link Paul forges in Romans 15, the most important missions passage in what is arguably Christianity's most important theological document. Romans 15 is the soaring description of the glorious worldwide mission of the church. And who is the cross-cultural missionary par excellence? The Lord Jesus Christ, who became a servant to a people and culture not his own. That's Romans 15. Romans 14, as we saw in the previous chapter, is about how to handle mundane church disagreements about scruples. What could these two topics possibly have in common? Yet Paul forges an unbreakable connection between them, a connection that will help us become more effective churches, evangelists, and missionaries.

The link comes in Romans 15:7, where Paul summarizes everything he has taught since Romans 14:1 about getting along with people in your church who have different scruples. Notice the key connecting word "For":

> Therefore welcome one another as Christ has welcomed you, for the glory of God.
>
> *For* I tell you that Christ became a servant to the circumcised to show God's truthfulness, in order to confirm the promises given to the patriarchs, and in order that the Gentiles might glorify God for his mercy. (Rom. 15:7–9a)

Do you see the connection? Verse 7 tells you to learn to love and welcome and submit to and reach out toward those in your church who are different from you. Why? *Because* (v. 8) that's what Jesus did when he left heaven to be born as a Jew, to become a servant to the Jewish race and culture so that the whole world could be saved.

Becoming a Good Little Jewish Boy

Instead of saying, "Christ became a servant to Israel" or "to the Jews," Paul says, "to the *circumcised*." Why that particular word? To remind us that Jesus didn't just become a servant to a race or a language but to an entire culture with all of its expectations, rules, and traditions intact—circumcision being perhaps the most famous of them. And it wasn't just any culture; Jesus submitted himself to a culture that was famous world over for being unusually strict.

Ponder this. The Son of God, who was not a Jew (he "became" one), left his complete freedom in heaven and *became* a good little Jewish boy and then a good, law-keeping Jewish man. The whole time he perfectly obeyed the very laws that he himself had given at Mount Sinai—even obeying laws that he knew were temporary because he designed them to be temporary (e.g., don't eat pork, worship only in Jerusalem). The only laws he pushed back against were those that the Pharisees and others had added or completely misunderstood.

Jesus in his life practiced what he later preached through Paul in Romans 14. He became a servant to people who were very different from him. He submitted himself to a culture that was foreign to him. He welcomed Jewish culture. He fit into Jewish culture. He wasn't some counter-cultural hippy who railed against everything traditional. He wasn't a weird outsider or misanthrope. He went to synagogue with his parents, and he went to the temple when he was twelve. He regularly celebrated Passover and other feasts in Jerusalem. He rested on the weekly Sabbath and attended synagogue service. He became a servant to the Jews and their culture.

What did the Son of God purpose to accomplish when he, for the glory of God, voluntarily became what he was not—a servant to a particular culture that was not originally his own?

Let's back up to verse 7 and get the bigger picture. We'll number Christ's purposes in brackets within the text.[12]

> Therefore welcome one another as Christ has welcomed you, for the glory of God.
>
> For I tell you that Christ became a servant to the circumcised [1] to show God's truthfulness, [2] in order to confirm the promises given to the patriarchs, and [3] in order that the Gentiles might glorify God for his mercy. (Rom. 15:7–9a)

1. Christ showed the world that God is truthful. Christ's first purpose was Godward, to completely vindicate God's truthfulness. Had the Son of God not become a servant to a culture not his own, this would never have happened.

2. Christ fulfilled all the promises God made to the patriarchs. Think of all God's promises in the Old Testament, hundreds of them. Their fulfillment depended completely on Christ's becoming a servant to a culture not his own.

3. Christ brought the Gentiles into God's family. None of the four Old Testament promises about the Gentiles in the following verses (Rom. 15:9b–12)—one through the lawgiver Moses, two through King David, and one through the prophet Isaiah— would have come to pass had Christ not become a servant to a people and a culture not his own.

You and your church are living, breathing results of Christ's willingness to serve a culture not his own, to love people so different from himself. He tells *you* to do the same in Romans 14 and 15. Jesus preached (through Paul) what he practiced.

---

[12] (a) Technically, "to show God's truthfulness" is an adverbial prepositional phrase (NIV: "on behalf of God's truth") that gives us insight into Christ's purpose in serving the Jews. The following two clauses are purpose statements. (b) Theologically, all of God's purposes are also results.

Now It's Your Turn

Jesus was the first to practice it, the first to become a servant to a culture not his own. Next it was Peter's turn (see Acts 10). Then it was Paul's turn as he became all things to all men to win them to Jesus (1 Cor. 9:19–23).

Now it's your turn. Paul says to you right now, "Be imitators of me, as I am of Christ" (1 Cor. 11:1).

What happened when Peter obeyed Christ and became a servant to a culture most certainly not his own in Acts 10? *You* happened (if you're a Gentile Christian), since Cornelius's coming to faith was just the beginning of Gentile fruitfulness, a fruitfulness Peter could not even have imagined.

What happened when Paul obeyed Christ and became all things to all men? More fruitfulness among the Gentiles—a fruitfulness that has spread over the whole earth.

What's going to happen when *you* obey Christ and become a servant to the people inside your church who aren't like you, who make you uncomfortable—people you want to judge in your heart because they're not strict enough, or people you want to roll your eyes at because they're not free enough?

What's going to happen when you obey Christ and become a servant to people *outside* your church who differ from you and who make you uncomfortable?

What's going to happen? The same kind of fruitfulness that came about when Jesus and Peter and Paul laid down their lives in the same way. Unimaginable fruitfulness. And fruitfulness always brings happiness to the glory and praise of God.

7

A CLOSING PRAYER

A church is a cross-cultural laboratory for effective mission. If a church is unhealthy in its own culture, then the last thing another country in the world needs is for that church to reproduce itself in that other country. The problems would only multiply.

Paul calibrated his conscience for love and mission: he unselfishly gave up some of his freedoms in order to love fellow Christians and to spread the gospel to the nations. Can you imagine how edifying a church would be—both locally and globally—if it were filled with members who calibrated their conscience like Paul?

Guilty consciences wouldn't paralyze church members. Instead, church members would serve God with cleansed and clear consciences.

Church members wouldn't arrogantly and stubbornly refuse to educate their conscience. They would always remain open to adjusting their convictions if they were misinformed. They would wisely calibrate their consciences with truth and due process.

Church members wouldn't squabble over disputable matters. They would love each other unselfishly and unite to mobilize their resources to spread the gospel in their community and to the nations.

And so we pray:

Father, we thank you for giving us a conscience.

For those of us who have experienced your electing love, we thank you for what you've done to our consciences: clearing them, perfecting them, cleansing them, purifying them, washing them, purging them, sprinkling them clean.

Now would you grace us to maintain consciences that are good, blameless, clear, clean, and pure?

Please give us grace and wisdom to calibrate our convictions about specific matters of conscience so they might become more scripturally informed.

Please give us grace and wisdom to love other Christians when we disagree about matters of conscience.

And as we spread the fame of your name globally, would you help us wisely evangelize and edify others in different cultures?

We ask this in the name of Jesus. Amen.

Appendix A

SIMILARITIES BETWEEN ROMANS 14 AND 1 CORINTHIANS 8-10

SIMILARITIES	ROM. 14:1-15:9	1 COR. 8:1-11:1
Weak in . . .	faith (14:1)	conscience (8:7)
Food restrictions are causing problems.	14:2	8:1
Practice your beliefs with thanksgiving to the glory of God.	14:6	10:30-31
Don't cause a weaker brother to stumble into sin by your freedom.	14:13-14, 21	8:9-11
We "know" that all . . .	foods are clean (14:14)	idols are nothing (8:4, 7)
Don't destroy your brother for whom Christ died.	14:15	8:11
Food is not important in the kingdom of God.	14:17, 20	8:8
Seek the good of others.	15:2	10:24
The Scriptures give us warnings and examples.	15:4	10:6
Christ is our example of giving up freedoms.	15:7-9	11:1
Give up freedoms for the sake of winning both Jews and Gentiles, just as . . .	Christ did (15:8-9)	Paul did (9:19-23)

Table 8

Appendix B

CONSCIENCE EXERCISES FOR
CROSS-CULTURAL EFFECTIVENESS

We're providing these exercises to help missionaries and other cross-cultural servants work through the difficult task of bringing their conscience under the lordship of Christ. Like Paul, we all need to ask ourselves, what stays, what goes, and what's missing? The overlapping triangles below remind us that neither the missionary nor the local has a conscience perfectly aligned to God's will. When we compare conscience standards between two cultures and then with God's will (illustrated by the three triangles in figure 12 below), we see seven areas of conscience agreement and divergence. The *sizes* of the seven areas in figure 12 are not intended to convey meaning. For example, area 3, where all three triangles overlap, should be quite large, since the values and laws shared by the world's cultures exceed the differences.

Before we consider some specific examples of conscience agreements and disagreements, look at the triangles in figure 12 and try to think of examples in your own situation.

In our corner of Southeast Asia where I (J. D.) have lived and worked since 1994, these areas of agreement and disagree-

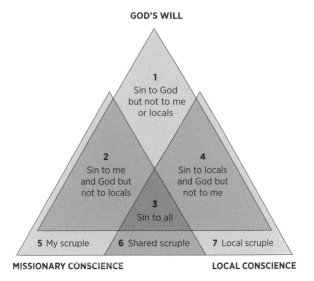

Figure 12. God's will, the missionary conscience, and the local conscience

ment get fleshed out like this. (Each number below corresponds with the respective area on figure 12.)

1. *God considers this a sin, but it doesn't show up on the conscience radar of either the missionary or the local person.* Many missionaries in Southeast Asia and nearly all locals have no qualms about purchasing pirated videos, though the national laws clearly prohibit such purchases.

2. *God and the missionary see these as sins, but not the local person.* For example, most locals have never even considered that a thought could be a sin. And they view idolatry as a virtue and drunkenness as something to be laughed at, not mourned. God has definite commands about all three of these issues.

3. *God, the missionary, and the local person all agree that these are wrong.* We could list many examples in this category. Most Buddhist countries have strict

Figure 13. God's will, the missionary conscience,
and the local conscience illustrated

moral rules against abortion, though abortions are
still common. Both the missionary and the local would
share convictions about this command and dozens of
others, such as those against adultery and theft.

4. *God and the local person agree that these are sins, but
   not the missionary.* As we saw in chapter 6, commandments about stinginess and care of the elderly are much
   more important in the local conscience than the missionary's, and they rate high on God's list, too (see, e.g.,
   Prov. 28:22; John 19:25–27; Eph. 4:28; 1 Tim. 5:8).

5. *Missionary scruples.* Though we in the West might
   try to make a biblical case against littering, the Bible
   doesn't specifically address the issue. It sure doesn't
   show up on the conscience radar of most people in the
   majority world.

6. *Scruples that both the missionary and the local person
   share.* Many missionaries in Asia have consciences that

don't allow them to consume alcohol, even though God's Word doesn't automatically condemn it as sin (Deut. 14:26). Most Buddhists in Asia share this rule, even though most of them commonly break it.

7. *Local scruples.* Every culture has its "sins" that God would not consider sins. In some tribes where I work, they consider it incest for two people with the same last name (clan name) to marry, even if they are not at all related. They also embrace many food taboos and other superstitions that do not bother Western missionaries and do not appear in Scripture.

Conscience Worksheet for Missionaries

To think further about these seven areas of conscience agreement and disagreement, consider the following questions. Which of the seven areas best match the descriptions below? (Answers may vary, and some questions may have more than one answer.)

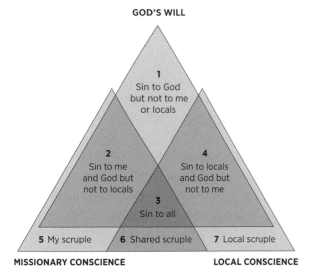

Figure 14. God's will, the missionary conscience, and the local conscience

1. On the day of judgment, God will likely judge the local person based *mainly* on infractions of rules in which area(s) of his or her conscience? _____

2. On the day of judgment, God will probably *not* judge the local based on infractions of rules in which area(s) of his or her conscience? _____

3. Day to day, the Holy Spirit convicts the local based on infractions of what area(s) of conscience? _____

4. If you went to Germany as a missionary, picking a fruit without permission from a neighbor's tree would fall under what area(s) of your conscience? _____

5. What area(s) of sin will missionaries tend *not* to preach against? _____

6. In what area(s) of conscience will the locals judge the missionaries as having a glaring lack of moral virtue? _____

7. In what area(s) will the missionaries think they're displaying an excellent testimony to the locals, while the locals will actually be unimpressed? _____

8. Missionaries will see the locals' most flippant moral lack when the locals break which area of conscience rules? _____

9. Preaching on which area(s) of rules will find a strong response in the local person's heart? _____

10. But why will missionaries tend *not* to preach against area 4? _____

_____

11. Preaching against what area(s) tends to bypass the local person's conscience? _____

12. Is it legitimate for missionaries to preach against sins in area 2? _____

13. The Holy Spirit will not add his convicting power when we preach against what area(s) of rules? _____

14. Missionaries' careful adherence to which area(s) of conscience rules will impress the locals? _____

15. What scruples should missionaries consider obeying during their time in the new culture, even though they know they are not actual sins? _____

16. Which area(s) would be considered a sin for both missionaries and locals, even though God has no commands against it (or them)? _____

17. It is legitimate for missionaries to attempt to add what category (or categories) of sins to the conscience of the local listener? _____

18. It is illegitimate for missionaries to attempt to add what category (or categories) of "sins" to the conscience of the local listener? _____

19. What area(s) of conscience do local parents scold their kids about? _____ What area(s) of conscience do missionary parents scold their kids about? _____

20. In the early stages of evangelism, missionaries should generally preach against what area(s) of sin? _____

21. Preaching against which area(s) of conscience rules would bring (legitimate) charges of colonialism? _____

22. Directly after conversion, our discipling efforts should center on what area of rules? _____ After that? _____

Answer key (answers may vary): (1) 3, 4. (2) 1, 2, 5. (3) 3, 4, and possibly 1, 2. (4) 6. (5) 4, 7. (6) 4, 7. (7) 2, 5. (8) 2, 5. (9) 3, 4. (10) Because it doesn't show up as a sin in their conscience. (11) 2, 5. (12) Yes, missionaries may introduce new conscience categories that are legitimate sins, but the locals' conscience may not immediately validate that new information. (13) 5, 6. 7. (14) 3, 4, 6, 7. (15) 6, 7. (16) 6, 7. (17) 2 (and 1). (18) 5. (19) 3, 4, 6, 7; 2, 3, 5, 6. (20) 3, 4. (21) 5. (22) 3, 4 first and then 2.

ACKNOWLEDGMENTS

I (Andy) am grateful to J. D. for coauthoring this book with me. His rich wisdom and life experience will serve readers in a way that I can't. I'm also grateful to my school, Bethlehem College & Seminary, for encouraging and empowering me to research and write in order to spread a passion for the supremacy of God in all things for the joy of all peoples through Jesus Christ. And I thank God for my godly wife, Jenni, who has given me more feedback than anyone else on this book's content and tone.

I (J. D.) am thankful to Andy for his wisdom, kindness, and patience toward me as we penned this book together, separated by ten thousand miles. What a privilege to work together with him. My leaders at EMU International gave me support and time to complete this project. Dr. Joseph Pipa, President of Greenville Presbyterian Theological Seminary, encouraged me in my early explorations on human conscience. My wife, Kim, is my best editor and critic—and dearest friend.

We would also like to thank Justin Taylor for offering incisive feedback on an earlier version of this book. Several others also reviewed the manuscript, which is all the better for their comments, including Brad Baugham, Brent Belford, Danny Brooks, David Crabb, Sam Crabtree, Chuck Hervas, Scott Jamison, Matt Klem, Dan Miller, Charles Naselli, Tony Reinke, Adrien Segal, Julie Steller, and Kristin Tabb.

GENERAL INDEX

SCRIPTURE INDEX